ODESSA 1919

REVIEWS

Odessa 1919 The Red Terror is an excellent read. The book is superbly crafted. The escape of the family mirrors our collective backgrounds, shedding light on conditions post WW1. A historical biography, it reads like a novel and is a page turner. One senses a future movie. Ronald French is engaging, his effort and detail are compelling.

Rich H., USA

This is a fascinating read. Both as a story and as an historical record. The Author's mother was a 9 year old child when, with her family, she fled the Bolshevik [Marxist] takeover of the Odessa area 100 years ago in 1919. The book is highly informative with maps and contemporary photographs. From a wealthy landowning family, with maids and a chauffeur, their pre-revolutionary, privileged life and customs are described in some detail. The horrors of the treatment at the hands of the CheKa or secret-police after the communists arrival are also vividly described. The difference between the promised paradise and harsh reality of socialist tyranny is apparent with every page of this book and should serve as a warning for those who are again being hoodwinked even today. The eventful and at times harrowing flight from Odessa to eventual safety makes for a compelling read. Recommended reading.

Harry Coe Bean, UK

This book is not only informative, but gives one a great understanding of what families had to endure 100 years ago to survive. A time in history that may not be understood by many in todays world. They for sure should read "The Red Terror" Thank you to the author.

Curious, UK

Odessa 1919 The Red Terror is an excellent read. The book is superbly crafted. The escape of the family mirrors our collective backgrounds, shedding light on conditions post WW1 . A historical biography, it reads like a novel and is a page turner. One senses a future movie. Ronald French is engaging, his effort and detail are compelling.

I bought this for my father and his review of the book is as follows:

Rich H. USA

This is a wonderful book, a quick read, and a historical masterpiece. It covers a little-known yet highly significant period – an axial turning point when the fervor of the Russian Revolution spread rapidly but sporadically south, eventually to the famed and beautiful Black Sea port city of Odessa. There, the Red Army and its supporters clashed over and over again with the emerging counter-revolutionary, pro-Tsarist White Army of Denikin. Recurrent violence accompanied the struggle between the two forces and their followers, engulfing local residents in a crescendo of murder. For well over a year, no one knew who would win, the Reds or the Whites. Who would survive, and who would be murdered, depended on the vagaries of the day. Statues were built, unveiled with great hoopla, only to be later covered up, painted over, revealed again, torn down, and re-constructed.

How often have times like this appeared in modern history?

To sociologists, the main if latent motif of this true story is the presence in Odessa, 1919, of what is called "anomie," i.e., normlessness. We follow the exciting story line as the main character, Paul Vaatz, had to switch personalities repeatedly over many months in order for him and his family to survive physically. Luckily, he was fluent in languages and cultures; apparently, he was able to adapt effortlessly.

In a larger sense, this is also about the dramatic end of a major social movement, one which had reached, at its apogee, a total of about two and a half million people. Invited by Russian rulers, and offered self-government (for the most part), religious freedom, and no military obligations, many farmers had emigrated from Germany to Russia, especially Southern Russia, beginning in the late 18th century. Paul Vaatz's grandfather was one of those geographically mobile farmers who moved south from Prussia in 1805, into the Black Sea region of Russia. Dedicated, hard-working, religious and upright, these settlers brought new techniques of farming to that rich region (now part of Ukraine) and, rather quickly, the German Colonies of the Black Sea Region became highly successful. They soon generated a number of wealthy landowners, as well.

As a result, many of the Vaatz family had moved onto their now landed estates by the late 1800s, to huge plantations they were able to purchase in the region to the north of Odessa, to conduct their farming. But the protagonist in this drama, Paul Vaatz, was sent to Western Europe to study business at a Belgian university. There he encountered the new Mercedes vehicle. Entranced, he went to Mercedes Benz at just the right time, as the company was planning to expand internationally. Awarded the agency franchise for Odessa, he soon had built a thriving business.

Paul and his wife, and their two daughters, settled into a luxurious apartment not far from the Mercedes office and across from a beautiful park, with views of the sea. During summers the children vacationed on the family estate. The book describes life on the estate for the girls, as visitors; the layout of the huge estate, its economy, daily life (especially during the warm days of summer) and the society of those who worked there. Serfdom was abolished in Russia in the 1860s, and so these workers were paid.

Then came the Kerensky Revolution, followed by the October Revolution. Bolsheviks sought to rid Russia of its aristocratic and backward past; the bourgeois population were among those designated as enemies of the people.

Into Odessa flooded the Whites of the Denikin Army, the Reds of the Russian Army, Ukrainian nationalists, and militaries from four foreign countries. From January of 1918 on, there were eight successive changes in the armies occupying Odessa. Paul and his family barely survived the horrors visited on others by the Cheka (the early Secret Police of the Soviets); they escaped with their lives to the countryside, saw and participated in a war between the residents of the German colonies and the Red irregulars, ran further west, toward the River Dniester, and, barely escaping, returned to Odessa when the Whites came back to power.

Paul realized, when many of his fellow bourgeois Germans did not, that the days were numbered for their sort of people in the south of Ukraine. Luckily, the family of Paul Vaatz obtained passage on the last boat allowed to leave Ukraine with those repatriating to Germany during that time. They arrived in Germany early in 1920 and when the girls grew up, they married two brothers, and both settled in Britain. One was the mother of Ronald French, the author.

Thus came to an end a historical movement that had yielded a set of colonies that thrived two centuries.

I've just read a memoir of the late Rosa Dranov, a brilliant Yiddish actress who grew up, partly in Odessa, terrified of the depredations of the Denikin men with their bloody axes, avoiding frequent death threats from the deeply antisemitic population of that region. Hundreds of thousands of Jews were killed during that time, mostly by the Whites and later also by the Reds; my own grandparents fled that bloody and tortured region during the vicious pogroms twenty years earlier.

People on all sides suffered; after all, violence, ignorance, bigotry, and class hatreds were hallmarks of the contesting forces during the civil war in southern Russia. The story told in this brilliant book describes not only the Red Terror of that time, but also the sad end to a brilliant two centuries run for a thriving culture these colonists had been able to create in their highly successful southern sojourn.

Joseph S. Drew, PhD
Editor-in-Chief, Comparative Civilizations Review, USA

Such a fascinating read. I loved it. Couldn't recommend it enough. I have bought it for several friends and relatives as a Christmas present.

Mallory Launchbury, UK, 28.12.2019

ODESSA 1919

THE RED TERROR

RONALD FRENCH

Early edition published 2018
French, Ron (2018) "Odessa 1919," Comparative Civilizations Review: Vol. 78 : No. 78 ,
Article 9. ISSN: 0733-4540
Available at: https://scholarsarchive.byu.edu/ccr/vol78/iss78/9

Copyright Ronald French 2019

Cover illustration after a painting by Ivan Vladimirov (1919)
Cover design, the author

To the memory of story tellers
Tamara and Isa

All this happened

100 years ago

Sadly, much the same still happens today

Frontispiece

The Khodinka beaker

The name 'Blood cup' is often used for this beaker because of the deaths its distribution caused. It was issued as a free souvenir at the coronation of Tsar Nicholas II in 1896. Huge crowds gathered at the Khodinscoe Fields outside St Petersburg to receive the enamelled beaker together with free food, a scarf and other gifts. In the excitement the crowds became unmanageable and many were pushed into the deep drainage ditches that crossed the level land. Over a thousand died. The tragedy was interpreted, by the superstitious in Russia, as a bad omen for the coming reign of the Tsar.

Contents

Foreword 1

Prologue 3

Chapter 1 – The Red Terror 14

Chapter 2 – In the CheKa 26

Chapter 3 – May Day 1919 39

Chapter 4 – Alexander Park 49

Chapter 5 – Eviction 57

Chapter 6 – Marazlievskaya 70

Chapter 7 – Deadly sailors 77

Chapter 8 – Bolshevik Guard Post 81

Chapter 9 – Grossliebental Cemetery 87

Chapter 10 – Grossliebental Murder 91

Chapter 11 – Towards Kleinliebental 96

Chapter 12 – Battle of the Villagers 100

Chapter 13 – West to Franzfeld 106

Chapter 14 – Jewellery Bag and a Snake 115

Chapter 15 – The Firewood Pile 120

Chapter 16 – Back to Odessa 132

Chapter 17 – At Karlovka 140

Chapter 18 – Baba Yaga 161

Chapter 19 – Revenge 169

Chapter 20 – Café Franconi 174

Chapter 21 – Too long in Odessa 179

Chapter 22 – The steamship Arta 192
Chapter 23 – Christmas Eve 204
Chapter 24 – Hamburg 209
Chapter 25 – Last Chance 214
Epilogue 221
Tailpiece 226
List of Illustrations 228
Acknowledgements 230
Sources 233
General reading 238

Foreword

Names are a nightmare

Between 1900 and today, many towns, villages and streets will have had three or more names; pre-revolutionary Tsarist, revolutionary, post revolutionary and then Ukrainian. In addition, all these might be written in Russian, Ukrainian, Anglicised or Germanic versions.

I have tried to use the names current in the 1900s, using an anglicised Russian. As this is a story of the past, I write Odessa rather than today's Ukrainian Odesa. I write of Russia, which it was in 1900. Ukraine, of course, remained part of Russia until well into the Communist era.

Both Germans and Russians love to use diminutives. And they will mix the two languages, thus Pavelchen; Pavel being the Russian for Paul, and –chen being a German diminutive. Names have variations that seem to be used at random, even in official documents, thus; Sophia, Sofia, Sonia, Sonya or Sophie. The Germans are no better, using both Carl and Karl, which can become Carlushka, -ushka being a Russian diminutive. For German names I have stuck with the German spelling. You will need to keep track of two Uncle Alberts, one Paul's oldest brother and the other the husband of Paul's sister Julia. Oma is German for grandmother, or Nannie, and is what the young girls called Sophia's mother, Friederike Kundert. Tante is German for aunty and Aunty Mathilde is often called Tante Tilla. You will quickly learn in the Prologue why this story of Russia has such strong German connections.

We also have the confusion of dates. When the Western World changed to the Gregorian calendar, Orthodox Russia retained the old Julian calendar. The Gregorian date is 13 days later than the Julian. When the Bolsheviks took power they also converted to the Gregorian calendar. In this memoire the old Julian system is used for 1919 dates and the Gregorian for 1920.

Feedback

Both Ebooks and paperbacks can be corrected and amended following publication, so please do feed-back errors and comments. I don't yet have a blog. Let me know if I should.

email me at: RonaldFrench1919@icloud.com

Do you want to continue reading in the train? Why not get the Ebook as well? Some of the illustrations are in colour. You will find it on Amazon next to the paperback.

Do let me know what you think of the story and please do review on Amazon.

Prologue

This prologue summarises the events leading up to the crisis that overwhelmed Paul, his wife Sophia and their two young daughters, of twelve and nine, in the spring of 1919. If you, my reader, are impatient to know the survival story, go straight to Chapter 1. You can catch up with the pre-history, later.

Paul's ancestor Friedrich Christian Vaatz, wife and two sons emigrated to the Odessa region in 1805, in the reign of Tsar Alexander I. They travelled from Merseburg in Prussia by horse and cart, as there were no railways at that time. They were among the first farmers to introduce the new breed of Merino sheep from Germany to Russia. They were provided with a free wood-and-adobe house, candles, dried cow dung for heating, an income of fifty roubles per month, flour, meat, a vegetable patch and a hundred *velro*[1] of vodka per year! They could not drink this all, and an early source of extra income was the sale of this vodka. They were also guaranteed a high degree of self-government, religious freedom and had no obligation for military service.

They immediately started to save and to buy land that was very cheap at the time. By Paul's generation, in the late 1800s, there were ten under the name of Vaatz, a number that ignores the estates belonging to female descendants of the line. The expansion-minded immigrants took advantage of the less responsible members of the

---

[1] Russian for bucket, an official measure equal to 13.12 liters. It appears that the good-living Evangelical immigrants received far more vodka than they wished to consume.

Russian aristocracy who sold off tranches of land to settle gambling debts incurred in fashionable cities such as Moscow, St Petersburg, Paris and, especially, Monte-Carlo. When Alexander I abolished serfdom in 1861 the German landowners ensured that their freed farm workers had proper accommodation, fair pay and a plot on which they could grow their produce.

A somewhat far-fetched story the German sheep farmers liked to tell, to demonstrate their growth and influence, was of their most successful countryman, Prince Falz-Fein, one of the few who had been ennobled by the Tsar. He was said to have been travelling in a coach to Saint Petersburg with the Russian Prince Esterhazy. Esterhazy boasted that he had 5,000 fine Merino sheep. The German prince congratulated him but would not reveal how large his flock was. After continuous pressure from his fellow passenger, he responded that *he* needed that many sheep-dogs to guard his herd.

Sophia's family, the Kunderts, arrived even before the Vaatzs. They were part of the first wave of immigrants, during the reign of Catherine the Great in the 18th century. The empress was an empire builder who had recently won territory from the Ottoman Empire. As a former German princess, she sought experienced farmers from her homeland to colonise and develop the land near the Black Sea.

The Vaatz and the Kundert families were close. They met initially due to business, Friedrich Carl Vaatz as one of the largest German estate-owners, and Johann Kundert as the senior mayor of the Liebental group of German colony villages. The smaller farms were situated here. The two men's paths frequently crossed at the various committees concerning German colony governance, where land rights, rental costs, education and product pricing were all determined. They sat on the management boards of the community banks and loans, schools, church and charitable organisations for waifs and the unemployed. A significant role was interceding with Russian government officials. Such meetings were usually held in Odessa but also in Grossliebental, the capital colony village of the several settlements in the Black Sea area within roughly 100km of Odessa. The two men's respective wives also met, be it at special ladies' events or dinners, related to both business and social activities such as the theatre, music, the arts, tennis and country walks.

Those colonist families, which had succeeded in expanding from being small village farmers to being the owners of large farm estates, typically spoke three languages; German as it remained the working language of the farms, Russian as the language essential for administration and business, and French to communicate internationally and to establish their status in relation to the Russian landed gentry. Having reached a degree of parity in wealth and landholdings, they aspired, also, to social equality. And, in general, their wealth did give them entry to the upper echelons of Russian business and social society.

In 1881, a year before Paul was born, it became compulsory to teach Russian in the village schools. One of Johann Kundert's (Paul's future-father-in law) more difficult tasks in this year, as a senior member of the school board, was to dismiss those staff that could not, or would not teach in Russian. At this time the colonists also lost two other important privileges, those of exemption from military service and the payment of taxes. Religious freedom was retained, although proselytising among the orthodox community was still forbidden.

Friedrich Carl Vaatz's oldest son, Albert married Johann Kundert's older daughter, Mathilde, and Friedrich's third and youngest son, Paul married Johann's younger daughter, Sophia. Mathilde and Sophia came from Johann's third marriage. Johann's first two wives died through illness, possibly in one of the many cholera, typhus, diphtheria or flu epidemics that swept through the region in those years. He also had a son, Waldemar. Both the fathers, Friederich and Johann, died early, before the start of the First World War. Paul's older sister, Cornelia married Albert Linke and a second older brother, Carl married Julia Esslinger. The Linkes and the Esslingers were also large landowning families. (See family tree at end of Prologue.)

Paul had a happy and contented early life on his father's Schastlivka estate 150 km north of Odessa. Similarly to his older brothers and sisters, he was given private tuition by the family governess. His father was strict but fair and insisted that his children become competent in all three languages. Paul enjoyed the life of the wealthy, took an interest in the working of the farm estate, in animal husbandry and the economics of the farm. He accompanied his father and older brothers on shoots almost as soon as he could walk. He was given a lightweight shotgun and shot his first duck at just fifteen. However, he was more academic than his siblings.

When his father died, at the tail end of 1899, although it was custom for the youngest son to inherit the estate, he agreed with his older brothers to take a smaller share of the land. Instead, he received funds that allowed him, first to study and then to establish a business. He and Sophia were married on the 18 September 1905 by Pastor Alber in the colony village of Grossliebental, where her father held high office. This was only three months before Odessa suffered the trauma of the Battleship Potemkin uprising. The following year Paul and Sophia travelled to Hamburg for the birth of their first daughter, Tamara. Whether this was because things had not yet settled in Odessa or for health reasons is not clear. He had planned to re-name the estate he had inherited, 'Tamarisa.' However, so close to the Potemkin episode and in the chaos of later years, this never happened.

Paul and family 1914. Tamara, Paul, Sophia and Isa are not a happy family. War with Germany has just been declared. There are rumours that they will lose their property and could be sent to internment.

He studied for a business degree at the University of Antwerp. While travelling in Europe, he was impressed by how the motorcar business was developing, especially in Germany. He negotiated with the early Mercedes Company to open an agency in Odessa, for this novel and rapidly growing form of transport. Soon after gaining the exclusive agency, Paul moved with Sophia from the family estate to an apartment in Odessa. There, in 1910, they had their second daughter, Isolde, invariably known as Isa.

The declaration of war, in 1914 pitted the Allies of Russia, Britain and France, against the Central Powers of Germany, Austro-Hungary and Turkey. It disrupted life in Russia and was a disaster for the German colonists; of which there were some two and a half million in Russia. All immediately came under suspicion. Although the Tsar proclaimed the confiscation of the German colony estates following the declaration the war in 1914, it was a bureaucratic process in which the property was to be 'legally' acquired by the government Land Bank at a ridiculously low valuation. The outbreak of the revolution in 1917 halted the process; so many estates were never formally transferred. Instead, if they had disgruntled workers, their owners faced internal insurrections, take-overs and even murder. On other estates, where relationships were good, both workers and owners were initially content to carry on more or less as usual in the hope that the situation would improve. The Vaatz estates experienced relatively few problems in the earlier years and the few unhappy employees generally left to make trouble elsewhere.

Many prominent ethnic Germans, including some of Paul's extended family, were interned in Ufa, a town 2,500 km northeast of Odessa. Paul faced a dilemma. Which side should he champion? Like many long-standing immigrant families, his instinct was to support the Tsar against his ethnic homeland. Russia was the only home he had known. Everything he owned was here. He was not interned, possibly because he had Russian citizenship and it probably helped that he had influential Russian friends in Odessa.

In 1917 the Bolshevik Revolution erupted in St Petersburg. This added to the misery of the ethnic Germans in the country. The confusion created by two simultaneous conflicts, gave rise to many competing power groups. These included the White Tsarist and the opposing Red Bolshevik revolutionary forces but also the Anarchist Black Army and the Greens. The latter being a militia made up of Ukrainian and German farmers seeking to defend their villages, animals and crops against the various armed bands that raided them for supplies. Also, there were the armies of Poland, Ukraine, and other Eastern European states, seeking to obtain their independence in the disruption caused by the Great War and the Revolution.

War Bonds. In 1915 Paul demonstrates his loyalty by investing large sums in war bonds. Vouchers, cut from these bonds, show that he tried to claim the 5% interest right up till 1919. It is doubtful, however, that in the chaos then taking place in St Petersburg, that he received these last instalments.

At the end of 1917, the Bolsheviks gained control of the revolutionary side and occupied St Petersburg and Moscow. Under Lenin, the Bolsheviks agreed to a peace treaty with Germany and its allies. Lenin's agreement, made against the wishes of many of his fellow revolutionaries, allowed the Bolsheviks to concentrate on their internal war against the Tsarist forces. However, this only added to the confusion. The accord enabled the German troops, during early 1918, to take control of most of Eastern Europe, including much of the Ukraine and Odessa, itself.

While the German occupation made life much less dangerous for the ethnic German population, it did not last, and their troops started going home already in November 1918, after Germany lost the war to the Allies. During the German occupation Paul volunteered himself as an interpreter but then sought his demob, again to allow him to remain with his family. He believed that the Whites could still gain the upper hand. This was not an idle hope as Anton Denikin the White Russian general had established a strong base only a few kilometres to the east of Odessa on the River Don.

His allegiance to the Tsar weakened as the civil war progressed and he realised that using his German citizenship, which he had maintained, could be helpful in avoiding arrest and execution by the Bolsheviks.

From January 1918 Paul's family had to suffer the hiatus caused by eight successive changes in the forces that occupied Odessa, both friendly and enemy. The city being intermittently held by the Red Bolshevik Army, the White Tsarist Forces, Ukrainian Independence Forces, the German Central Powers (Germany and Austro-Hungary) and the Western Alliance (Britain, France, Greece and later America).

By early 1919, the families of three of Paul's estate-owning close relatives; brothers Albert and Carl from Karlovka and Schastlivka, respectively and brother-in-law Albert Linke from Cherson, had all chosen to come to their *pied-a terres* in town. They had wrongly assumed it would be a secure centre of White power.

When the Reds succeeded in occupying Odessa, for the second time in April 1919 all families faced the risk of arrest and execution by the CheKa[1] secret police. This creation of Stalin's viciously hunted down the rich, the intellectuals and all the ruling classes, in a holocaust-like campaign of extermination known as the Red Terror.

---

[1] CheKa' from Che and Ka, the Cyrillic first letters of *Chrezvychainaya Komissiya*, translated as the Extraordinary Commission to Combat Counter-Revolution – synonymous with terror.

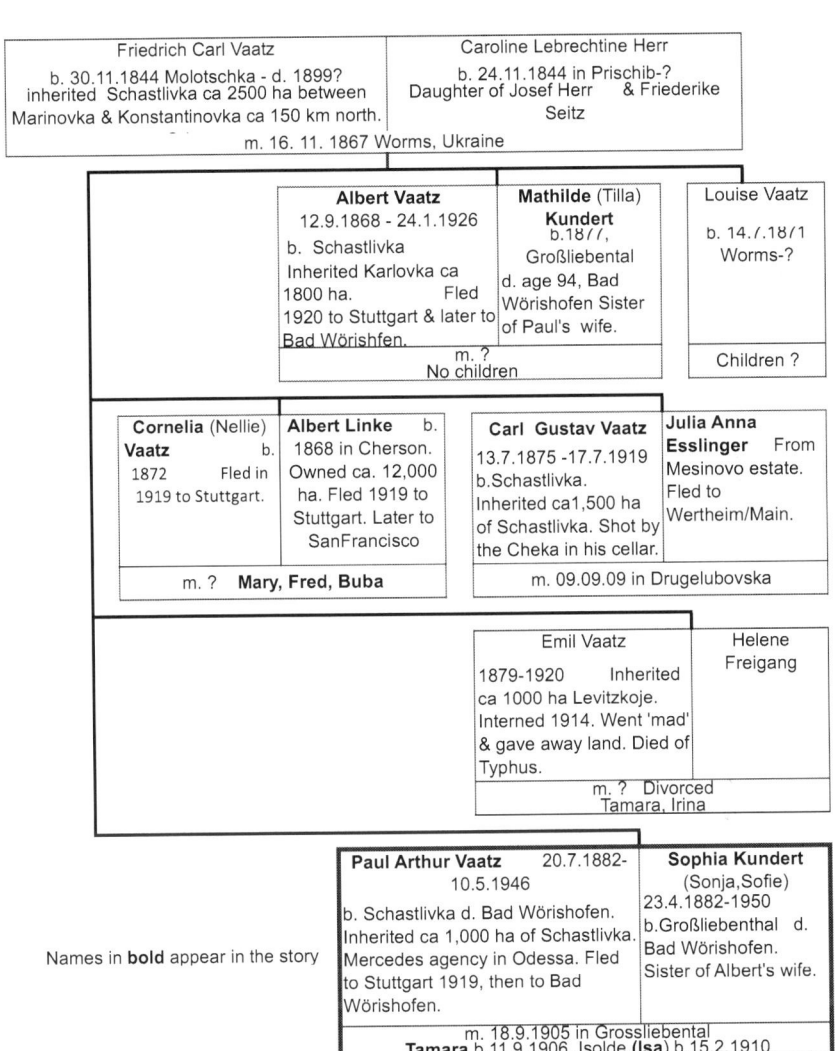

The Vaatz Family Tree

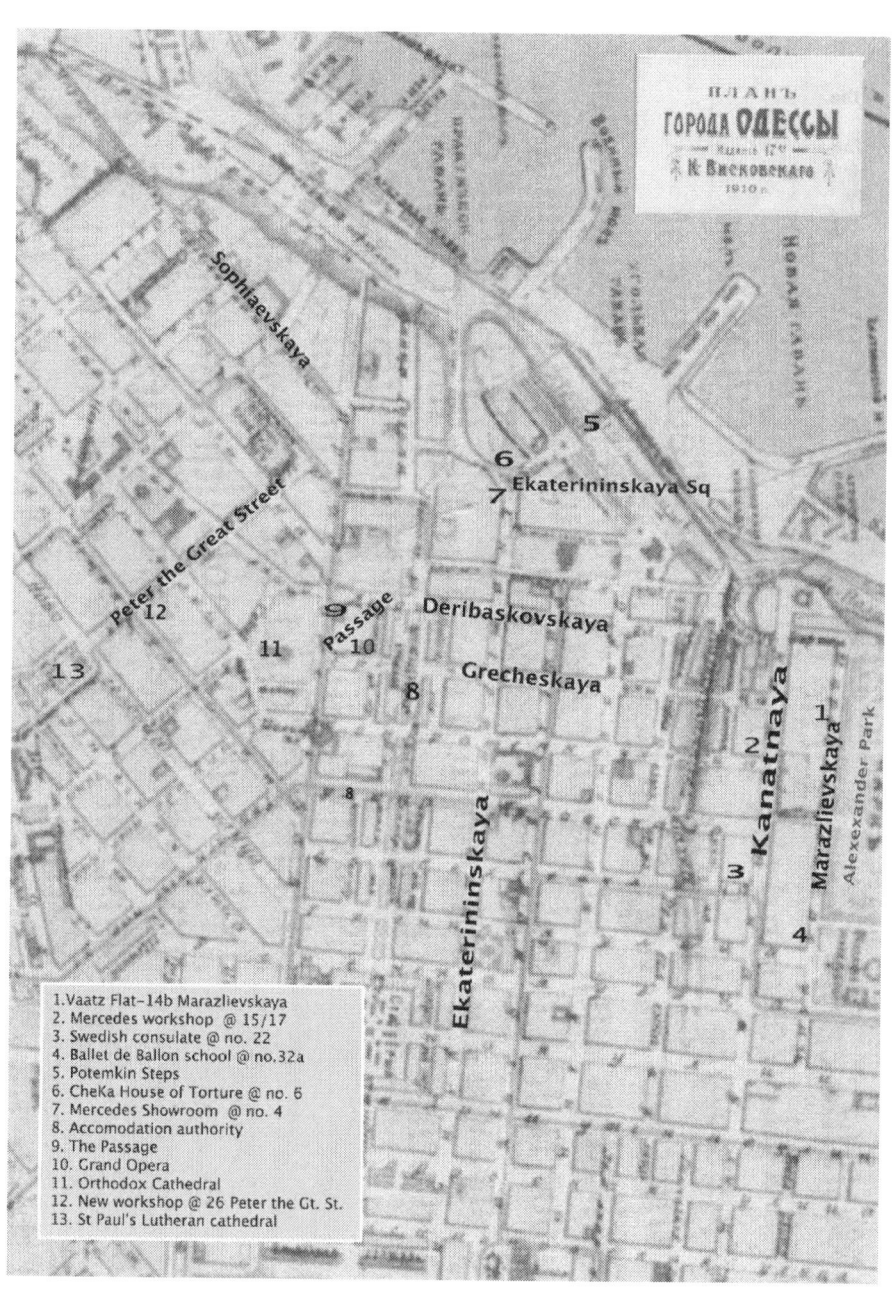

1910 plan of Odessa showing key streets and locations.

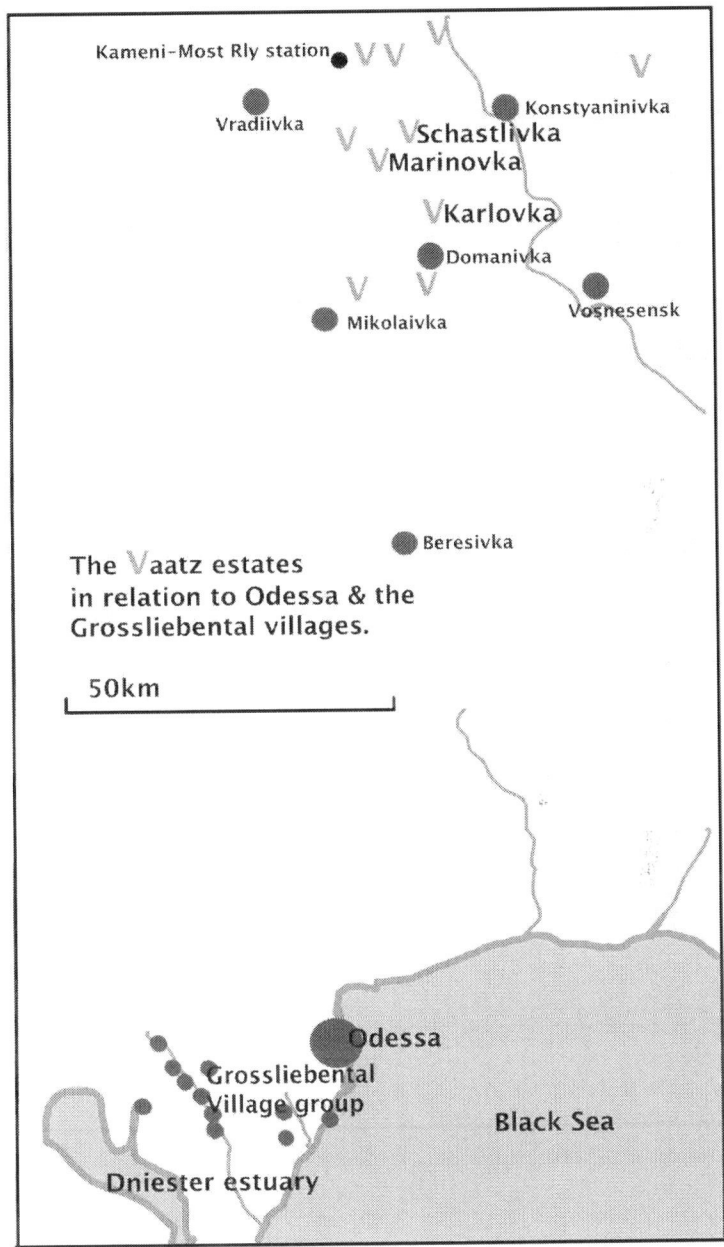

The Vaatz farming estates, Odessa and the Grossliebental group of German colony villages.

Chapter 1 – The Red Terror

Sophia is sleeping. Paul is restless. His gaze follows the movement of car headlights reflected on the bedroom ceiling. There is a screech of tyres, and the movement stops. Heavy boots hammer on the marble of the apartment block's central stairway. Orders are shouted, a heavy banging, two gunshots. The door of the flat below crashes in. A pause, then a desperate woman's howling plea. Again the sound of boots in the hallway, getting fainter, the slam of car doors, again the screeching tyres, then a frightening silence. Sophia now is wide-awake. Both listen. Nothing.

'God, the CheKa![3] Poor, poor, Irma,' She shudders, 'They've arrested Igor.' Paul pulls her close. They both know Paul could be the next.

They had talked about the danger of arrest as soon as the Bolshevik Red Army had entered the city a week ago, shortly after the departure of the final contingent of Allied troops from Odessa on the fourth of April 1919.

The CheKa's reputation for cruelty and ruthlessness had arrived ahead of it. Stories of arrest, torture and execution in St Petersburg and Moscow are spoken of in fear. All who hold positions of responsibility are wealthy or intellectual are at risk. No proof or evidence is necessary to justify arrest.

---

[3] CheKa' from Ch and Ka, the Cyrillic first letters of Chrezvychainaya Komissiya, translated as the Extraordinary Commission to Combat Counter-Revolution. The Bolshevik secret police, synonymous with terror.

The CheKa is ruthlessly scouring Odessa for those they deem to be enemies of the State. These they drag to their newly requisitioned headquarters, in the Zhdanov building at Ekaterininskaya Square, 6, for incarceration, interrogation, torture or execution. The Bolshevik gazette, *The Fight,* routinely announces the fate of the victims with the reason for arrest typically and coldly given as *Counter-revolutionary and informer,* or something similar. In their hunt for victims, the CheKa encourage their own informers and are working through the records in City Hall. So, while Paul is not an official of the city, he will be exposed as a wealthy landowner and businessman as soon as the Red commissars uncover his files. The threat is real and close.

Paul accepts that he and Sophia have been in denial, hoping the threat would somehow go away and reluctant to leave their luxury apartment overlooking Alexander Park and the Odessa harbour. They have been stupid. His own and perhaps all their lives are at risk. They must escape the City, get to the villages outside and become anonymous. So far, they have done nothing. Now they must, and soon.

In the morning, Sophia goes down to see what she can do to help and comfort her neighbour. She feels guilty she hadn't gone down the moment Igor Dychenko's abductors had left. She and Paul had been selfish, worrying that the CheKa might return for him. Sophia volunteers to look after Irma's children so that she can concentrate on trying to achieve her husband's release. It is faintly encouraging that a few have already managed to have their loved ones freed using contacts, bribery, influence, or whatever corruption worked. Again Sophia has a bad conscience for, even as she is consoling Mrs Dychenko, she finds herself scheming what she would do if Paul were arrested. Her mind is confused and in a panic. How much worse must Mrs Dychenko feel?

***

With the Bolsheviks storming the city on the fourth of April, the family had not thought to celebrate Easter when it came only three days later. This happy, momentous day in Russia had been entirely ignored amidst the terror and death of the invasion. Sophia is still shocked at what has happened to the Dychenkos, but she does not want her fear to spread to the two girls, so she cheerfully proposes they should catch up with Easter. It is impossible to bake the customary *Paska* (Traditional Ukrainian Easter cake) as there are no ingredients. However, she does have half a dozen eggs, smuggled in from the country. These she hard-boils and gives to her young daughters, Tamara, twelve, and Isa, nine, to decorate. For a while, there is silence and intense concentration as the work progresses, interrupted by a little argument over who is to use a particular colour. They cannot dye the eggs as is traditional, so they have resorted to their box of paints. Sophia makes black tea, and the grown-ups admire and praise the artistic efforts of the girls. There is welcome laughter and pretended offence at the surprise portraits of Mama, Papa and Mademoiselle.

Papa complains, 'Goodness I don't have a big nose like that!'

They have an egg each and then play scissor-stone for the odd one. Papa wins and tries to give it to the girls, but they insist that he and Mama must share.

Even last year, in 1918, they had still managed to hold open-house at Easter. Russian neighbours and friends and German relatives all came. The atmosphere had been a little strange and strained, as the German Army was in control of the city at that time, while the Bolsheviks and the White Army were busy fighting each other further north. But the Vaatz's friendship with their long-standing Russian friends was stronger than both the nationalistic rivalry between their two countries and the political conflict within Russia. All guests had been happy that there was at least peace and order and hope for a better future.

Isa tells – Easter before the Bolsheviks

Tamara and I love Easter. In Russia, it is even more important than Christmas. Before the nasty revolution spoiled everything, we two would walk to *Sobornaya Ploshad* (Cathedral Square) and sneak into the Orthodox Cathedral of the Holy Assumption for the Easter morning service. In the dark height, gold sparkled everywhere reflecting the lighted candelabra above us. I wondered at the two candles by the altar, taller than I and thicker than my arm. Gold-framed icons of the saints covered the marble altar screen, St Peter, in red with his keys to paradise and Saint Mary in blue and white, praying with eyes looking to heaven. The larger than life paintings around the wall, telling the story of Jesus and the passion, were a bit frightening and made me sad. Little bells rang as the priest and servers, dressed in gold and white came chanting down the aisle with the server swinging his smoking censer to the left and right. We tasted the strange, sweet smell. The chanting was in an old Russian we could not understand, and the singing of the male choir made my spine tingle. Nearly everyone stood. Only the very old rested on pull-down carved dark wooden half-seats fitted to the walls. The carvings were in the shape of grotesque faces both human and animal. The rich ladies showed off their furs, and the men held silk top hats to their front. (I naughtily thought it looked as if they wished to pee in them.) The peasants and workers stood heads bowed, women in headscarves, men holding their cloth caps. Then there were other Russian-Germans and foreigners, and we nodded and smiled to those we knew. Although we found it mysterious and fascinating, we never managed to stay the length of the full service.

A Ukrainian Paska

Our Ukrainian Paskas were baked two days before Easter. The kitchen had to be kept super-warm with no drafts to spoil the

required three separate kneadings and rises of the sweet yeast-dough, containing nuts and candied fruit. Oma (German for Grandmother) Friederike, Mama's mother, who lived with us, was in charge of the kitchen. She would be shouting at the two maids and at everyone else to keep the doors shut. She dressed all in black, and when she went out, she wore a black scarf. In the kitchen, Oma covered her black with a large pure white frilly edged apron.

Sometimes Tamara and I were a little embarrassed, in front of our more snooty friends, that she looked like a village woman and it was true that she did own a house in Grossliebental. However, I boasted that grandfather Johann was an important man, the head mayor of the Liebental group of villages, who had been awarded the prestigious title of Honorary Citizen.

The Ukrainian Paska is tall like a top hat (The Russians would call it a Kulich. They have an entirely different cream and sugar Paska of their own.) Our Paska is covered with a soft lemon and sugar icing that runs down the sides like snow and is usually decorated with a double-barred Orthodox cross, or with the Chi-Ro symbol of Christ. We coloured hard-boiled eggs using onion-skins to get red and brown and got other colours using powder-packets from Germany. We would shrug off the anxious supervision trying to protect us from dirtying our dresses or scalding ourselves. We polished the painted eggs with goose fat to make them shine and debated how best to arrange them around the Paska on the large sideboard in the dining room.

After morning church, Papa and Mama welcomed visitors. Many came. Our visitors were Russian and German friends and neighbours including the occasional consular official who would want to test our French. We were happy to oblige as we considered our French to be quite good. All were dressed in their best, including two army officers who arrived in full dress uniform. One even brought his sword that he stood in the hallstand alongside the umbrellas.

A few children came too, cousins, school friends, children of Mama and Papa's friends, who we didn't know very well, and neighbours. After 1914 I missed my best friend, Herta who had always visited with her family. They had been interned when the war with Germany started - Papa had to explain to me what that meant. They were sent to a town called Ufa, very far north. We sent each other cards, and in winter 1915 she wrote saying how much fun she was having in the snow, riding a troika and sledging. I asked Papa if we could go to Ufa, too. He just gave me a sad smile, patted me on the head and said it was not a very good idea and that I would not enjoy it.

Our visitors spread between the dining room and lounge and also the balconies if we were lucky with the spring weather. We served Paska, little *Piroshki*[4] and other small bites.

Strong Russian black tea was poured from the blue and white teapot, warming on the top of the large samovar, into tall glasses held in embossed silver holders. The samovar stood steaming in the corner, where there was a special flue with a hole through the wall to take the steam and smoke from the room. Because of the heat it produced, the samovar stood on its own white marble-topped table. It did not matter then if the odd piece of hot charcoal or ash fell upon it. Our guests had to queue patiently for their strong tea to be diluted with boiling water from tap on the front of the samovar. Guests helped themselves to lemon slices stacked in the bowl beside the samovar together with sugar, as most liked their tea very sweet.

Papa cut the *Paska* horizontally, into disc-shaped pieces, sliced into halves. The top was replaced to preserve the remaining cake and was the last piece to be shared out. This usually happened a day or two later, which was lucky for us, as it was our favourite because of the icing.

Although there were two maids in white caps and aprons, we also helped to serve. There was much shaking of hands and kissing. Three kisses, from one cheek to the other and back, and the greeting, *Christos Voskres* (Christ has risen,) responded to with, *Voistynu Voskress* (indeed He has risen.) There were uncles and friends and young men (still much too old for us) but some that we little girls quite liked kissing and others that we preferred not to. But once we were in sight, there was no saying, 'No.' The room quickly filled with

---

[4] Small savouries typically shaped like miniature Cornish pasties with a variety of fillings such as meat, herbs, egg and onion.

smoke as cigarettes in holders, cigars and pipes with long stems were all popular. I proudly offered cigars from a silver cigar box engraved to look like wood.

All took part in the *Chuck-chuck* competition with the hard-boiled egg that each had picked from the colourful display. The first round was knocking the narrow-ends of the eggs together, to see who had the strongest. Then our guests competed with their flat-ends in the same way. Finally, the winning narrow-ender and flat-ender went into battle to find the overall winner. There was much cheering and laughing, claims of cheating and some disappointment — no prize except yet another egg or a perhaps another Vodka.

Visitors would not stay long but move on to visit other friends. After everyone had left, we used to whisper between ourselves, who was the worst person we had to kiss. Tamara hated beards, but I quite liked them. I thought them manly. I particularly liked Uncle Volodia's who's was warm and smooth and not spiky like a brush.

Tamara and I enjoyed being in the kitchen. Oma could sometimes be a little fussy, but she spoiled us too. So long as we spoke German, she would allow us to stay. Sometimes, without her knowing, we would hide under the big table in the middle and listen to what was going on. We would get to learn bits of both Ukrainian and Yiddish. Ukrainian, because it is very similar to Russian and is what the servants, who were mostly from the country, spoke. Yiddish as it has bits of German and is what the Jewish tradesmen spoke when they came to sell fish and other fresh products. It was cosy and warm in the kitchen, and the tradesmen used to stay for a chat and were often given a glass of sweet Russian lemon-tea. We invented our own secret language that was a mixture of Ukrainian and Yiddish. Papa, who was keen that we spoke perfect French, was impressed with our creativity but thought it to be misdirected.

Isa tells – School

When I was five, I joined Tamara at the Ballet de Ballon private school. It was held in a room of the Ballet Academy only a ten-minute walk up our street, at 34a. It was very grand with wide marble steps and a huge glittering chandelier in the entrance hall. Thin, athletic dancers floated up and down those steps. Some who were very friendly to us little girls and chatted but others were condescending and looked snootily at us as if wondering what on earth we were doing there. We learnt more French, especially cursive writing. I made myself unpopular with our Russian French teacher by saying that her pronunciation was not as good as our governess's, Mlle. Voutaz. When I started school, because I was young, I was allowed to draw pictures in my story writing classes. I loved this as I got high marks and was disappointed when, later, this was no longer allowed.

Sometimes on our way home, we would-pay a visit to Papa's Mercedes motorcar workshop in Kanatnaya Street that runs parallel to our own. At numbers fifteen and seventeen it was not exactly on our way but only a bit of a detour If Papa was in and in a good mood, he might treat us for tea and cake down the street. If not, Herr Etin, the manager would politely greet us. He was friendly and from Germany and although he spoke a little Russian, our German was better, so we were happy to show off. He would let us sit in the cars and pretend to drive and introduced us to some of his staff.

We had long school holidays in summer, and when we were not in Karlovka, we often went to the beach at Lustdorf, another German colony village, on the Black Sea. It was only ten kilometres away from our apartment. There was a horse tram. Mama told me it was the same age as me and had started in 1910. It was noisy and rattily and looked fun, with passengers hanging on to the outside. But the grown-ups thought it too dirty and crowded, so we usually went in a hired carriage. If we went in one of Papa's Mercedes cars, it was really quick. He seemed to have a different car every time we went. We were told that this was because he was testing them or demonstrating different models to customers. Sometimes a stranger came with us to the beach for a test drive. As most customers were inexperienced, they drove too slowly or too fast or stopped suddenly, so we fell around screaming and laughing in the back. Often they could not start the car. If we hadn't taken a chauffeur with us, Papa had to do the hard work of turning the engine with a big handle. Papa got told off by Mama when she heard of our escapades saying it was dangerous and stupid, but we enjoyed it. This was strange because usually, it was Papa who was the careful one and Mama who liked adventures. Luckily Papa ignored her but made us promise not to tell next time we went. If our cousins came to visit us in Odessa we usually drove out in Papa's own big Mercedes that we called *Mamasha* because it could carry so many children.

In the Mamasha Mercedes. From the left: Mary Linke, Visitor, Tamara, Isa, Chauffeur Griffin, Fred and Buba Linke, Mlle Voutaz

In 1917 when I was only seven, Mama and Papa got news of the revolution in St Petersburg, but we continued to go to school. In February 1918 the German Army took control of Odessa from both the Bolsheviks and the White army, and school continued. But because we were Germans in a Russian school under German occupation, the atmosphere was a bit uncomfortable. Neither our Russian friends nor we knew quite how to behave.

The German soldiers started to leave already in November and were replaced by soldiers from France and Greece. The French troops were black, and they frightened Tamara and me. We had never seen black men before. Mama explained they came from Morocco in Africa, and there was no need to be afraid. There were English ships in the harbour. But these all departed in spring 1919. Soon after we could hear shooting in the distance but still went to school. Then one day on the way home, suddenly, we had to dodge from door to door to avoid bullets. Somehow we were not very frightened. It didn't seem real. No one would want to shoot us. But Mama decided we should have lessons only from Mademoiselle who always spoke in French. She both read to us and had us read from Bibliothèque Rose. She also taught us French songs that we enjoyed.

By April 1919 the Bolsheviks were already in charge again. Although there was almost no shooting Mama still said we had to stay indoors for our lessons. We could tell Mama and Papa were worried. Papa was stricter than usual, and then he was sorry and came and sat with us and asked what we were playing. Mama sometimes looked as if she had been crying. When it got scary, I got into bed with Tamara. We cheered ourselves up by saying Papa was clever and would know what to do. We had heard him tell Mama that because we were German-Russians and the German Army had made peace with the Bolsheviks, they would not dare to do anything nasty to us.

Chapter 2 – In the CheKa

Paul and Sophia are again awakened in the very early morning, by a loud banging. This time on their own door. Is it the CheKa for Paul? They get up, go to the door, shuffling in slippers and tightening their dressing gowns around themselves. Then they stand, terrified and undecided whether to open up or to try and escape by the back entrance. The door will be broken down if they delay.

But Sophia holds up a finger, turns her head, puts her hand to her ear to hear better and whispers, 'Listen!'

They both realise it is a woman's voice shouting and crying. Paul eases open the door to find a sobbing, hysterical Cornelia, Paul's sister and wife of Albert Linke. She tells them that he has been dragged away without any explanation other than murmurings of 'Bourgeois collaborator.' Sophia worries that Cornelia has walked right across town in the dark.

She holds her close and looks her in the eyes, 'You could have been kidnapped, murdered or raped.'

'Don't be silly Sophie.' Interjects Paul, "All that matters is how to get Albert out,' and to Cornelia, 'Come sit down. Put this rug round your shoulders.'

Sophia apologises and she and Paul try to reassure Cornelia that a way will be found to obtain Albert's release. This, even though neither knows how.

Paul's older brother Carl arrives, having been given the awful news, he had first taken Cornelia's children, who had been left in charge of a very frightened governess, to his wife, Julia.

They discuss intently and urgently what to do. It is urgent because many have been abducted one day and routinely shot the next. Others, they know, could spend months and potentially years under interrogation and torture. It is Carl who finally suggests a possible approach. He has learned that Herr Finkel, one of the Jewish maklers, who has acted for many years as a broker for the Vaatz brothers in the selling of wool, animals and corn from their estates, has reached a high position in the local Party. Carl had always found him to be honest and straight. Indeed, he cannot understand why Finkel is supporting the Bolsheviks. It has to be worth trying to contact him and to see whether he will help. Cornelia agrees and is firm that she, herself, must go and persuade Finkel to use his influence to free her Albert.

By the time they arrive at this decision, it is almost five in the morning and getting light. Carl accompanies Cornelia on her return walk across town. His apartment, in *Ulitsa Petra Velikovo* (Peter the Great Street) is close to hers in Sophievskaya. He reassures her that he and Julia will look after the children.

Back home Cornelia makes a strong coffee, sorts her valuables trying to decide how much a life might be worth and what she should take. It's too late to try and sleep, so she sits slumped in an easy-chair, staring into space. One minute she is firm and determined as to how she will manage the discussion and the next in quiet tears, imagining what Albert must be suffering and trying to dispel the thought that she might fail. At half-past eight, she stands at her door, takes a deep breath and sets off, planning to arrive before nine when she assumes the CheKa will be 'open.'

Do they have office hours just like a shop? She wonders and thinks it perverse.

This walk is much shorter than to Paul's apartment by Alexander Park. She goes towards the harbour, first left, right, right, then left again, into the curve of Sabanyev-Bridge. The once smart shops she passes are now shattered, windows smashed and looted out. All signs or fixtures incorporating the double-headed eagle have been torn down, defaced or painted red.

She enters Ekaterininskaya Square and there already are the Red Guards stationed in front of the Cheka building. She turns sharply right to avoid them. She is too early and needs to settle herself.

At the Ekaterininskaya Street exit from the square she passes Paul's Mercedes showroom, situated in one of the most prestigious locations in town. It has received the same treatment as the others. The three cars on-display have been vandalised and stripped. Cornelia assumes they have not been stolen, because there is no petrol left to run them. She leans against the wall of the show room and puts a hand on her heart. It is beating fast. She adjusts her hat, smoothens her skirt and looks at her watch. In exactly five minute she will go.

The famous statue of Catherine the Great still stands there but it has been hidden, under dirty white ragging, by the Reds. Only Catherine's bronze hand pokes out, pointing defiantly towards the West and to civilisation. Beyond Catherine is the Zhdanov building, now the CheKa headquarters and known locally as the House of Torture.

After passing the exit to the Potemkin Steps on her right, Cornelia finds herself shaking. Her journey round the square is complete and she can no longer avoid addressing the Red Guards. She will do anything and everything she must to achieve Albert's release.

Three black-leather uniformed figures stand casually at the CheKa entrance archway. Two, to the left of the entrance arch, are talking to each other. They have rifles, a holstered pistol and a sabre each. The other, on the right and with only a gun at his belt, is leaning against the wall smoking and has a clipboard dangling from his left hand. All look menacingly relaxed. Tentatively, she approaches the one with the clipboard. At first, he ignores her, doesn't listen or look until he hears the name 'Comrade Commissar Finkel.' She has to control herself to be as humble and polite as possible. He examines the tattered bundle of sheets attached to his clipboard, silently points her to the first door on the left inside the archway and gruffly gives her a room number but no floor and does not offer to help or accompany her. She explores through the building.

She was here with other members of the family when invited to the unveiling of Catherine the Great's monument nineteen years ago. It is very different now. Before it was grand, brilliant and bright. Now it has become dirty, dark and threatening. It even smells different. Does fear have a smell? She wonders, as she climbs the once-grand stairways and searches the long corridors, feeling exposed and vulnerable. She does not belong. Those she passes give her questioning, hostile stares, the women even more threatening than the men, but luckily no one stops her. She finally finds the door with 'Comrade Commissar Finkel', handwritten on a piece of card roughly inserted into a holder on the door. The holder apparently covers an earlier name and Cornelia pessimistically wonders whether the previous occupier is still alive. She knocks as resolutely as she can and enters when invited.

She recognises Herr Finkel immediately and he, her. She has spoken to him frequently on the estate. This was not on business, that was Albert's or the estate manager's role, but informally and politely when meeting him on his way to his overnight lodgings or perhaps going to a meal arranged for the many traders that visited in the season. He stands up as he recognises her, and both realise that this is not how a commissar is expected to greet a Bourgeois plaintive. He waves her to the chair by his desk and quickly sits down. He is dressed as a worker, in that he has a collarless shirt. But he is not scruffy, and evidently sees himself as a man of status in the new regime. There is a little red badge in his left lapel. Before the Revolution he had not been one of those Orthodox Jewish maklers, wearing long black coats with tall hats and payots hanging either side of their faces but had dressed as a western businessman. Like her, he speaks both fluent German and Russian and in the ensuing discussion, each uses the language that best suits the meaning. She wonders whether he can also understand French but then gets cross with herself for wasting time on such unimportant thoughts. In spite of the tension, Cornelia can't help thinking that at a different time, she would have been able to have a very civilised conversation with Finkel. He does not need to ask why she has come.

She has brought with her a small but weighty bag holding a dozen large solid silver dessert spoons to use as barter. They are part of her dowry and engraved with the initials of her maiden name, CK. She had assumed that Finkel would not want cash, as this was becoming more devalued each day. He examines the spoons and agrees they are valuable but then asks her politely to remove the pale grey glove on her right hand. He is interested to see the large ring that it covers. It has a prominent central aquamarine surrounded by small diamonds.

'I will arrange to have your husband released in return for this ring.'

'But it is a wedding anniversary ring from my husband.'

'That makes it a particularly appropriate exchange.'

'Will you not be shot if you are found with my ring?'

'I will cut it and sell it in pieces. But you are right I will be arrested and shot if I am exposed for, as you obviously know, it is illegal to speculate. I am careful and deal only with those I can trust. I will manage.'

'But it does not come off in any case.'

'So many "buts" Mrs Linke? Come, come, you wish to save your husband?'

Herr Finkel takes her hand as politely as he can to check the fit of the ring. She submits without objecting to this intimate action.

'Not a problem. We will cut it off. As I said, I will need to break up the ring in any case. I am doing you a kind of favour. If you do not want to be arrested, like your husband, you must never wear a ring like this again. You should not even wear gloves unless it is freezing and then wear practical gloves, not fancy, fashionable ones like these. You need to take off that big expensive hat now. Throw it in the corner there. I'll get rid of it for you. Best wear a headscarf or simple cap. Please wait a minute.'

Do I have a choice? She thinks as he leaves the room. She gets up and pulls a nearby chair along the wall to the corner he has indicated, removes two large hairpins and arranges her hat and gloves tidily on the chair, then sits down again with naked hands on her knees. He returns with a pair of small but sturdy clippers, probably intended for cutting tough toe-nails, and comes round the desk.

He glances at the chair in the corner. 'I'm sorry, but it is for your own good. I would not like to see you in the CheKa.'

Removing the ring is tricky because of its tight fit but, although he nips the skin, he manages without drawing any blood. He then notices the plain but wide gold wedding ring.

'I am prepared to return your aquamarine stone for that ring. The stone is really worth much more, but gold is more easily traded. What do you think?'

She tries to think clearly. Here she is bargaining for Albert's life. She doesn't care. Stone or gold just save him and agrees. The wedding ring slips easily from her finger, and she half rises from her chair, stretches forward and places it on the desk. Finkel uses the points of the clippers to prize the aquamarine from its mounting and reaches across to hand it over.

'We have a counter-revolutionary tribunal at three this afternoon. I am chairman, and we do not have many prisoners to consider.' He wraps the two rings in a wrinkled, spotted red kerchief and leans back on the legs of his chair to place it in the centre drawer of the desk.

'I'm reasonably sure I can arrange to have your husband released. I will make the case that he treats his workers fairly and has shown an understanding and sympathy for the Party's cause. He also has skills that can help the Party in its vital food production programme. Further, I will argue that we can keep an eye on him here in Odessa and that he should not be allowed to leave the city without permission.'

He guides her by the elbow to the window. 'Stand over there on the other side of the square,' and he points to the corner holding Paul's, now shattered, show-room. He notices her start. 'Yes, it is difficult, but times are changing, and you must learn to adapt if you are to survive.'

Paul's Mercedes showroom in Ekaterininskaya.

While she has noticed the showroom, another realisation has come to her; that she and Albert had stood at a window on this same floor in 1900 when Catherine's statue was being unveiled. She and Albert had not yet been married but he had secretly squeezed her hand when no one was looking. God, how I need him, she thought.

Finkel continues, 'Wait there this afternoon so you can see the archway below, soon after 3:30. If he does not come out by 4:30, or 5:30 at the very latest, you will know that I have failed. I then guarantee to return your rings. You will know from the past that I am an honest makler.'

It is a perverse bargain, but she believes him. She returns to their lodgings and spends the many miserable hours both worrying and at the same time trying to be as positive and optimistic as possible. That Sophia and Paul are not around is a blessing as she does not want their comforting at this time, and would rather see no one until Albert is free. She warms some borscht but can then hardly swallow. 'Why bother?' Time drags and then, in the end, seems to rush. She dresses down, as instructed and, in a headscarf, hurries to the allocated spot only just in time. Then this terrible, terrible waiting. 3:30 passes. It would have been a miracle had he emerged so soon. Then 4:00, then 4:30. Then 5:00! Tears start to come to her eyes. 'Have I really lost him – forever?'

At five past five a bedraggled, hunched figure emerges, tentatively as if lost. Cornelia sees him humbly present a document with two hands to the guard, who laboriously extracts a pencil from an upper pocket, scribbles something on his clipboard and then returns the paper. Albert creeps uncertainly away, looking nervously around. Cornelia rushes straight across the square, past the shrouded Catherine, and pulls him away, far from the entrance. They hug and cry together. Slowly they go home. This terrible experience is more proof that things are getting very dangerous for them all. Somehow they need to leave Odessa.

***

Albert does not tell Cornelia how terrifying his experience in the CheKa has been. Although he has not been physically tortured or interrogated but pushed around - each shove being accompanied by one of the several standard epithets used by the Bolsheviks: bastard, bourgeois blood-sucker, usurer, capitalist, informer, counter-revolutionary.

In Ekaterininaskya Square, his abductors had handed him over to two warders, one with a rifle slung in a strap over his shoulder the other with a holstered pistol. He was frogmarched through the central arch of number six and to a building in the large courtyard behind. There he was pushed towards a counter in the corridor and ordered to hand in his coat.

A cloakroom just like a hotel, he thought wryly, and his thoughts were echoed from the counter,

'Welcome to the Zhdanov, hotel for the aristocracy.'

The warders took his jacket and riffled through his pockets. He was then given it back. It only held a few low-value paper roubles that were pocketed by the two warders.

'I thought you counter-revolutionaries were meant to be rich.'

Albert did not attempt an answer. They demanded his braces.

'We don't want any suicides. The tribunal decides how and when you die. Best to cooperate and inform.'

He had to sign for his braces and top-coat. They did not record the money taken. Albert knew that Paul's Russian neighbour had been executed very soon after his arrest. He thought of Nellie and the children. That neighbour had had children too.

One of the warders unlocked a door to the left. There were stairs, and they escorted him down, one in front and one behind to a dimly lit cellar corridor. It must previously have been used for storage. Now there were numbered prison cells doors along one side. He started when there was a scream.

'There Sir, we like to make our visitors welcome.' This from the warder, behind.

They came to a door with number three roughly painted on to the door.

'Your lucky number, Sir.'

One warder unlocked the door the other shoved him in so roughly, he almost fell. The door slammed shut, and the lock turned. Albert stood shakily and looked around. The cell had probably before been used for storing coal. This would have been delivered through the hole high in the wall above that had been roughly boarded over. A single light bulb hung from the ceiling. A large square tin stood in the right-hand corner, and the room stank of faeces and urine. He felt sick, swallowing back the rising bile he debated with himself: how had they managed to change a luxury block of apartments into this place of filth and horror?

By the left corner, two men sat on a thin layer of straw with their legs pulled up against their chests. One had dried blood on his face and hands, and his shirt was bloodied and torn. He held his head in his hand and was moaning quietly. Albert shivered as the reality of the hell he had entered pressed on him. The second prisoner struggled up. He showed no signs of bad treatment and had on a warm jacket.

'Greetings comrade.'

'Good day,' Albert answered cautiously. 'What happened to him?'

'I assume he did not co-operate. What are you in for?'

'I have no idea.'

'Come, come. You must have done something. I was caught selling my gold watch, which the silly bastards called speculating. You must have broken one of the new regulations.'

'Not that I am aware of.'

'Good answer. Ignore the provocateur!' That coming quietly from the rocking man on the floor.

The man opposite continued, 'Well they'll tell you soon enough, and you had better agree, or you'll end up like this poor chap, or worse.'

Albert decided to close the conversation and sat down against the wall, somewhat apart from the other two. He needed to think. I must have been dragged out of the house at about three in the morning. So now it must already be six or seven. What will happen next? He knew it would not be pleasant. At intervals, there were more screams and cries of varying urgency and intensity.

The door opened. A warder stood guard; another pushed in three bowls plus three slices of black bread. The door slammed shut again. Albert, as the most agile, got up and presented two of the tin vessels to his fellow prisoners. The injured man whispered a polite reply, and his hands shook as he took the bowl. The other grabbed the offering and immediately put it to his mouth. Paul then settled to test his breakfast. There were no spoons, so he drank as if from a cup. He imagined it was meant to be a soup, but it was thin, thin, thin. No salt, no meat. Someone might have briefly shown it a cabbage leaf, he thought. The bread was a little better. At least it was solid.

The small shutter in the door could be opened from both inside and out, and it was evident that the CheKa wanted prisoners to see how others were treated. It was a planned part of the 'cure.' Through this square port-hole, Albert recognised one poor man, who had been marched out walking tall, later being hauled back to his cell, head hanging low and arms pulled tightly around the shoulders of the warders each side of him. His feet trailed uselessly behind. He could have been dead. But Albert thought not, For why bring him back, then?

Throughout the rest of the day, there were more screams that left those locked up to imagine what was happening. There were several shots, but Albert could not tell whether this was simply to frighten or whether each shot was an execution. Initially, he started each time he heard a shot, but then he didn't. They became part of the general background noise of despair. How quickly such terrible sounds can become commonplace.

In what Albert judged was the middle of the afternoon, there were shouts and commotion outside. Albert got up, meaning to look through the viewing hatch, but he jumped back, as the door was suddenly slammed open. Prisoners were ordered to stand by their doors and to watch and learn. Armed guards stood along the facing wall. Three blind-folded men were already kneeling on the stone floor. A guard, dressed in black leather, decorated with several red flashes and stars, strutted behind the three kneeling victims. Albert assumed he was a CheKa commissar.

'This is how we punish counter-revolutionaries and enemies of the state.'

He moved behind the first and shot him in the back of the head. The shattering sound in that confined space echoed through Albert's brain. The victim slumped sideways, blood and bone spattered onto Albert's shoes as the head smashed onto the stone floor. Albert shook uncontrollably. As the commissar positioned behind his second victim, number three collapsed. He was ignored, and the second victim shot. The executioner indicated with a nod of his head and the command *'Skoro!'* (Quick!) and two warders righted the third victim, grabbing the cloth around his shoulders. He, too, was shot. Paul's stomach cramped, and he bent double as he was pushed back into the cell. He was ready to vomit. If the intention was to frighten inmates into submission, it was effective. Albert did not watch, through the hatchway, as the corpses were dragged away. He had had enough.

He sat against the wall, like his companions but a little apart, his head in hands, and waited. He worried about Cornelia and realised he was moaning and rocking like his fellow inmate. This will not do; he told himself and stopped the rocking. There were yet more screams and shots, but sadly, Albert thought, one almost got used to them. What else could one do but wait? He waited for a long time, trying to be positive, but it was not easy, whether thinking about his own future or of darling Nellie.

Then there was a key in the lock, and the door opened.

'Albert Vaatz stand forward! Come!'

He rose to his feet slowly, with great effort, like an old man and received a sarcastic, *'zhelayu tebe udachi'* (Russian - 'I wish you good luck), from the provocateur.

There was an incomprehensible mumble from the other that Albert felt was well-meaning. But as the two warders marched him along corridors, his fears grew. Where to? To interrogation, to torture?

He was taken back up the stone cellar steps, one guard leading the other following. The one behind cursed and pushed his rifle-but into the small of Albert's back when he stumbled. Out in the open yard again, Albert realised he was shuffling along with despair. He thought 'To hell with them,' straightened and made an effort to walk normally. The two guards guided him through the inner court yard like a farm animal with a push from one side and then a shove from the other, all accompanied by appropriate curses. He was being taken towards the exit archway. 'Are they going to transport me? Where to? It can't be worse than this place.' They stopped. One warder handed him a crumpled but official-looking piece of paper. He saw a red star at the top and a signature at the bottom. Did he recognise the name, Finkel?

'Show this to the guard at the gate. Lucky bastard, you are free. And you'd better keep this with you as proof you are legitimate.' Said, one warder.

But from the other, 'Lucky this time but don't crow. You'll need to stay in town, and we'll have you back again for good, very soon. They all come back and next time bribery won't help.

Albert stumbled out through the archway, presented his paper to the disinterested CheKa guard and looked wildly around him. Cornelia came running.

Chapter 3 – May Day 1919

The First of May arrives. The Reds have been in the City a terrifying month, and Paul has still not found a way to leave. The streets are dirty and full of litter. Shop fronts have been smashed in. Scruffy, self-important Red officials, walk the streets wearing red armbands, pistols at their waist and bayoneted rifles slung over their shoulders. These are now the police. Anyone with any previous high status creeps around in fear. All dress as poor workers. The disguises have to be good. Some will have rubbed dirt into fingernails, and others have even used glass scraps to make their hands look used. It would be a comedy if lives were not at risk.

Sophia is bored with being cooped up and, in spite of the danger, persuades Paul, they should go to Ekaterininskaya Square, named after Catherine the Great and with her statue standing proudly at its centre. Sophia wants to watch the Bolshevik May Day celebrations that are certain to be taking place there. She argues that she and Paul will be less obvious mixing in with the crowd.

Paul ponders that he has already experienced three versions of an enshrouded Catherine the Great. His first, long ago, was joyous, on the sixth of May 1900, the birthday of Tsar Alexander II. Paul had especially taken a short break from his business degree studies in Antwerp. The Zhdanov family, who owned the impressive building at number six, the square, had invited the Vaatzs to the formal unveiling of the new Catherine monument. They had a privileged view from a top story window. At that time two neatly draped pure white Tsarist flags had hidden the statue, and when the Tsar pulled the golden chord, these had fallen away to the sound of trumpets and the cheers of the crowd. There were speeches and music, royal gun salutes and the national anthem.

Grand inauguration of Catherine the Great monument, 1900.

It was on that occasion, he had started to take a real interest in Sophia and to think how beautiful she was. Up till then, she had just been the younger sister of Mathilda, brother Albert's wife. On that day, as they watched the ceremony from the window, Sophia had blocked his view of the royal unveiling, and he had an excuse to put his hand on her shoulder asking to see better. She had half turned to see who it was and moved aside. During the champagne afterwards, they chatted. This turned into an exchange of letters and postcards after he had hurried back to Antwerp.

His second viewing came when the Reds had first stormed into Odessa in January 1918, following their earlier triumphs in St Petersburg and Moscow. They hid the empress from view with nasty grey canvass ragging, crudely tied with rope. The CheKa commandeered the Zhdanov building as their Odessa headquarters at this time. In the intervening eight years, before the Bolshevik occupation, the building had been modernised and a story added by the Zhdanov family.

In a happy reversal, the third time was when the German Central Powers threw the Reds out again in March of the same year, as they took control of much of Eastern Europe, in *Operation Faustschlag* (Operation Fist-strike) Paul got this third viewing when he rushed to welcome and congratulate the triumphant Austro-Hungarian troops as they entered the square and tore down the insulting Bolshevik coverings.

Victorious Austro-Hungarian troops. Removing Bolshevik wrapping from Catherine the Great monument. February 1918.

Today, nineteen years after his first viewing, as he and Sophia creep into the square from Ekaterininskaya Street, they find Catherine hidden from view, yet again. How many more times will she and the population of her sorry city have to experience these dramatic and frightening changes? Paul wonders.

However, 'On this occasion......,' as Paul cynically comments to Sophia, '....the Reds have made a big effort.'

May Day 1919. Note the caricature of the Bourgeois in his top hat on the right.

Someone has cut out crude wooden stars, painted them red and hung them on the dirty shroud like Christmas tree decorations. A big red flag spreads out in the breeze above the centre of the Zhdanov building's colonnaded roof. A huge banner, stretching along the whole front of the building shouts the message, *The Provincial Emergency Commission for Combating Counter-Revolution, Speculation, Sabotage and Other Offences*. In other words, *Beware, we are the CheKa*. Paul takes a perverse pleasure in noting that the golden Zhdanov cartouche still shines brightly in the sun, above the massive red star the Reds have stuck on the building. They have not yet figured out how to remove cartouche. A brass band plays stirring revolutionary music.

Paul and Sophia find a place, behind the main crowd, where they can lean unobtrusively against the wall across from the Zhdanov building. This is not by his ransacked Mercedes showroom, which would pain Paul and where someone might just recognise him but on the other side of the entrance to the square. They face each other and grin. Paul looks like his chauffeur when in his scruffiest car-maintenance outfit. He has removed his gold-rimmed glasses, carries a walking stick and stoops. He has made sure his hands and fingernails are dirty. Sophia too has roughed up her hands, no gloves, of course, wears a cheap red, decorated cotton headscarf is in flat-heeled, scuffed shoes from the kitchen and in a worn, dark brown coat.

Paul looks across the square at the insulting defacement of the once beautiful building and shudders at the atrocities that are said to be taking place there. It is rumoured that the CheKa organisations in Saint Petersburg, Moscow and Odessa competed with each other as to which could invent the most gruesome methods of torture. Odessa's trademark torture was said to be the tying of their victims to a plank and feeding them gradually into a furnace or boiling water. Paul hopes that Sophia hears nothing of these stories. He certainly has no intention of frightening her with them.

***

Sophia brings to mind how, only three months ago, on the 17th February, they had also stood at the back of a crowd, not far from where they were now waiting, and watching a very different scene; the funeral procession of Vera Kholodnaya, the World famous Cinematographie silent star from Odessa. The Ukrainian National Army had then been in temporary control of Odessa and gatherings had been forbidden. The troops had been uncertain how to deal with the excited but peaceful crowd that formed to watch the funeral procession. Wisely, the commander ordered his men to stand back and not to interfere. There was much crying, and mourners pressed forward to touch the open coffin and if they could, the body of the actress. Sophia couldn't understand why mourners risked getting so close and even touching the body. They could easily catch the disease themselves. The mint that the undertakers scattered on the corpse was no protection, and she did not, in any case, like its sweet smell. Sophia remembers how sad she had felt that the flu pandemic had killed someone so young and talented, but it was not a personal loss that had made her wish to cry. She just felt relief that the pandemic that year had not affected anyone in her own household.

She had seen Kholodnaya act and remembers the first time when, one day four years before this funeral, Paul had arrived from work and told her that they had received a surprise invitation to a chamber concert, that same evening. It was within walking distance in a block further down their road. Number six or eight, she recalled. She had had to get ready more quickly than usual, although Paul said it was not formal and he had kept on the suit he had been wearing in the Mercedes showroom. They entered the small but elegant concert room, decorated mostly in white, with gold-gilded plaster decoration. The chairs were also gold gilt with red velvet seats, and Sophia was glad that she had taken the trouble to dress appropriately.

There was a pretty little stage that would have accommodated, perhaps, up to ten orchestra members but no chairs for them to sit on; only a big white sheet hung at the back. In the central aisle between the two sides of the auditorium was a contraption, that's all she could call it. It was a peculiar machine with a light inside and with two wheels, one above the other. She looked at Paul. He just said it was a surprise, wait and see. The lights went out, and there was a murmur. Sophia was not the only one who was being surprised. Then the machine started, and the words, *Flame of the Sky* appeared on the sheet above the stage. Next came the name *Vera Kholodna* and also other names. The machine whirred, and figures appeared. They were moving and gesticulating! There was a gasp and mutterings between partners. It was unbelievable. Sophia clasped Paul's arm. The story was of the illicit love of a young woman married to an older man and rather sad. Sophia watched unbelievingly at what she was seeing and, in spite of the technical novelty, still became engrossed in the story. It was also Paul's first viewing and, although it had been explained to him what he would see, he was still impressed and wanted to understand precisely how the magic had been achieved.

***

So much for the crowds of the past. They must return to the reality of the present. This is provided by the man who comes and leans against the wall beside Paul, interrupting both Paul's morbid - and Sophia's more nostalgic - thoughts. He wants to chat. Paul does not.

'A great day for the Revolution, hey comrade?'

'What?' says Paul putting his hand to his right ear but with his stick still dangling in the 'V' between fingers and thumb.

'A great day for the Revolution!'

'Ah, yes. Long live the Revolution!'

Are you from town? This from the man.

'What?'

'Are you from town!?'

'This is Odessa.'

'I know, I know. Are you from ..... never mind. I'm from Tatarka.'

'You're a Tatar? You've come a long way.'

'No, no. Forget it. Do you know where I can get some bread?'

'You know where to get bread? Wonderful. Explain to my wife; she hears better than I.'

The stranger gives Paul a look, wondering whether to continue but the loudspeaker crackles and Paul stabs his stick meaningfully towards the staging. The man leaves them to find someone else to pester. They stay a while listening to the propaganda, the promises being made of free land and plentiful food, and the frightening words of hatred against the Bourgeoisie and the threats of death. Sophia shivers as she senses the force of that hatred. She cannot understand from where it has come. They raise their fists and cheer with the crowd but then leave quietly, when it seems safe to do so without appearing unpatriotic. On the way home Sophia scolds Paul for his theatre, she says it was all she could do to stop laughing, and that would have been disastrous. Paul retorts that at least the little charade ended the questioning.

An awful scene awaits them when they return. They find Irma Dychenko looking dazed, sitting on the cold marble steps of the apartment, just inside the street door, Hugging her two children close to her knees. They are gazing up at her; their looks both questioning and frightened. She silently reaches up and hands Sophia a page torn from the infamous Bolshevik gazette *Borjba* (The Fight) that a neighbour has just left her. Paul and Sophia see Irma's husband's name, circled in blue indelible pencil, fifth down in a list of twenty city officials. All were executed last evening. Against each name are repeated the words: *Bourgeois city official and counter-revolutionary.* That is their crime! So quickly, so soon. No appeal, no official letter to the wife. She had not been able to seek out any useful contacts. On Sophia's advice, she had first tried to speak with Comrade Finkel but the guard at the CheKa building would not listen and would not let her in. Sophia feels hollow inside. The poor woman. How will she survive, how look after her children?

The dependents of so called guilty counter-revolutionaries are not recognised as citizens, not even as people. They receive no ration vouchers. They are not allowed to work. Anyone providing informal work for payment is also punished. Sophia has already seen other widowed wives begging on the streets. But anyone offering to help has to be careful not to be seen by one of the many Red officials patrolling the streets. Sophia invites Irma up to the apartment, and prepares some hot borsht and cuts generous slices of good rye bread she has been saving. She also finds some chocolate for the children who nibble tentatively. Irma accepts the nourishment with polite thanks but with listless fingers and eats because she knows she must but finds it difficult to swallow. Sophia feels at a loss that she can do nothing more helpful and practical.

As Paul watches how lovingly Sophia is caring for Irma and her children, he realises how important it is for he himself to survive, for without him Sophia and his two lovely girls will be in precisely the same tragic situation as Irma. It just must not happen.

Chapter 4 – Alexander Park

Later that month, Paul goes to the bedroom balcony, as he always does when he first gets up, to breathe the morning air and to absorb the view. Not so long ago he used to think how lucky the family was to live in such a modern apartment block, overlooking Alexander Park and the Odessa harbour beyond. This morning his feelings are confused, still pleasure at the beautiful view but real fear as to what might happen to his family.

He recalls how, after their marriage, he had felt the need to be based in Odessa near his Mercedes business, so they had rented an apartment at number sixteen Marazlievskaya, where their second daughter, Isa was born. They liked the location and two years later managed to become the first apartment owners in the new block of flats just being completed next door, at Marazlievskaya, 14b. It was on the second floor and had central heating with running hot water, electricity, and was one of the first in town to be fitted with lifts.

A flurry of spring air blows from the harbour, through the rustling park trees and over the balcony. Paul pulls his dressing gown more tightly around him. Sophia smiles as his uncontrollable quiff of fair hair is whipped up. She feels safe with him. We will find a way out of this mess together. He is tall, and she admires his straight back and falls in love again. She had been right to say, 'Yes' in 1904 when he had proposed as they were celebrating his graduation together.

Holy Trinity 21 May 1901. Picnic at the Marinovkaya estate, between Schastlivka and Karlovka. Annotated by Isa, in the 1950s. *Aunt Olia* is not in our story. Principals are: *Tilla* (Mathilde), *Mother* (Sophia,) *Nelly* (Cornelia,) Paul's sister seated on ground. Paul lying in his new student attire. *Grandmother*, Friederike Kundert is mother of Mathilde and Sophia.

For someone who was usually quiet and reserved he had been very forward earlier, in 1901, when they were together at the picnic on the Vaatz's Marinovka estate. His three traditional Russian kisses had been more passionate than was proper. Taken by surprise she had neither rejected nor responded but parted, she imagined with a bit of a blush. She had looked round to see if anyone had noticed. Her mother was turning away with a little knowing smile on her lips. Was this an arranged meeting? She had wondered.

She remembers how she had worn a new white silk blouse, ordered by her mother as a present from Hamburg. A decorative silver buckle held her long dark green skirt. Older sister, Mathilde was dressed very similarly except that her skirt was a navy blue. This hadn't been arranged, and they often laughed when they arrived at gatherings to find that they had both chosen very similar outfits. They were very close. Paul had appeared, proud in his new student outfit, complete with peaked cap. She had warned him not to get involved with sabre duels and had made it clear she didn't consider a scar across the cheek would enhance him in her eyes.

Paul breaks into her thoughts. 'What on earth is going on? Vadim and others are down there dancing around like idiots, and a Red Army rabble is streaming across the park to the harbour.'

'So? Get dressed. Go and find out.'

Paul changes in a rush and, too impatient to wait for the lift, bounds two steps at a time down the marble stairway, sliding his hand along the polished wood-topped iron bannister. He emerges from the apartment's central archway and hurries across the road. His friends are not dressed as workers. What on earth is going on? He wonders. Vadim has on his fashionable red-lined cloak, and a red, silk waistcoat, showing a stand-up collar and a large bow tie. Alexander is in a long black topcoat with top hat and sporting a blue silk cravat. Paul knows a pearl-tipped golden pin will be holding it. The other two have also dressed as if they were going for a Sunday stroll in the old days. Something must have changed if they are all so confident they can do this without being arrested as counter-revolutionaries.

'Fantastic news, Paul! Look, the Bolshies are running scared. General Denikin and his army are marching into town. We'll soon all be free again.' This from Vadim, his Russian lawyer friend.

The other three give Paul enthusiastic two-handed shakes and hug him close. Alexander is pumping his silver-topped stick up and down, holding it at the bottom like the Drum Major of a marching band. The others are throwing their hats high into the air. All are equally excited and jump around and cheer. Their enthusiasm infects Paul, and he joins in. Grown men, laughing and dancing around together, arm-in-arm, like silly schoolboys in the playground.

From behind comes a sneering, threatening voice, 'Cheer and jeer while you can you bourgeois scum! Our great Red Army is simply making a strategic retreat. It'll be back, and when it does, we shall shoot the lot of you and hang you by your legs from these trees, like the dogs you are.'

A broad-shouldered, tall young man with red hair emerges from the trees behind, wearing a scruffy, long grey army great-coat with the regimental and rank markings torn off - a sure sign to the friends of either a revolutionary or a deserter. He brandishes an extended shiny, brass-bound telescope as if ready to beat them with it. All five stare in stunned silence.

However, Paul, realising that the initiative is now with them, turns on this spoiler of their celebrations. He slowly takes a clean white handkerchief from an inside pocket, shakes it open, removes his glasses and carefully polishes them.

As he replaces them, while squinting sideways at the red-head, he demands, 'And where the devil did you manage to steal that expensive telescope?'

The Bolshevik steps back, hugs his telescope close, pats it lovingly and replies in an offended but proud tone, 'This is not stolen, it's been requisitioned for the benefit of the people.'

Next to have a go is Paul's short, portly friend, the Russian lawyer. He makes the intruder jump, stabbing two stretched fingers into his stomach. 'You take great care what you say, young man. I can have you arrested, tried and almost certainly shot for words like that.'

The Bolshevik's face shows fear.

But that look does not last. It turns slowly into a cruel smile as he stares, at first questioningly then excitedly beyond the little group. He barges suddenly through them towards the road that edges the park, where a small troop-carrier, holding half a dozen Red Militia, has just appeared.

He yells as he runs, pointing awkwardly backwards at the friends so that he almost trips. 'Comrades, quick, come. Come shoot these blood-sucking, bastard Bourgeoisie.'

The militia tumble untidily out of their open truck, weapons awry, trying to understand what it is the Bolshevik wants. At first, the friends just stand and stare. Then, realising the danger, they shout to each other to run and hide. Alexander Michaelovitch is stuck, staring rigid with fear; his silver-topped stick planted firmly on the ground. Paul grabs an arm and drags him into hiding.

Vadim, instead of running with the others further into the park, takes the suicidal decision to run left at an angle towards his apartment, further along the same road from which the militia is shooting. All are terrified he will be killed as they watch the bullets hit the ground behind him. Somehow, perhaps because of the confused shelter created by the park trees or the marksmen's lack of training and skill, the bullets miss their target. The friends are relieved to see the lawyer's small round figure, with his black, red-lined cloak flying behind, dive into the entrance-arch of his apartment block to safety.

The remaining four stay crouched behind a fallen log, screened by bushes. The gun-fire, urged on by the excited shouts of the Bolshevik, is now directed at them. Many shots come close, thudding into the fallen tree where they are sheltering. Paul ducks instinctively as a bullet ricochets off the top of the log and over his head. However, the aim is somewhat random, for in trying to murder the lawyer the militia have not seen exactly where the friends are hiding. The lawyer, by risking his life, has possibly saved theirs. But they are not safe yet.

There is silence. Why? Have the gunmen already entered the park? Have they spread out and are stealthily stalking their prey? Are they getting close? They can't hear the Bolshevik. Is he urging them with silent signals? The uncertainty and fear increases. The friends crouch low, remain still and listen for the sound of rustling grass or a broken twig.

Alexander, the one who had been frightened rigid before, can't stand the tension and starts to straighten from his crouch to look out. Two friends pull him down; another warns too loudly that he will give them away, Paul whispers not to shout. All are panicking. Alexei, in spite of the warnings and the tugs on his coat, manages to see out and to the horror of the others screams, 'Look, look!'

Realising that their location is now revealed all raise their heads. They are astonished to see the militia scrambling onto their transport, even as it starts to move towards the harbour. At first, they wonder, why the panic? But it is quickly apparent that the gunmen fear they will be at the mercy of Denikin's advancing army if the ships in the harbour leave without them.

Relieved, supporting each other and shaking from shock, they stumble out from behind their log. Paul's family hurries towards them from the apartment block. His younger daughter, Isa, runs ahead with arms held wide. Sophia and Isa's sister, Tamara, are half walking, half running hand-in-hand. Mademoiselle Voutaz, the governess, follows, hands clasped together, uncertainly behind.

'Paul, Paul, we saw everything from the balcony. It was terrible, awful. Thank God, you are all safe.'

Paul sweeps up the dark-haired Isa. As Tamara, with her long fair hair, arrives he moves Isa to his left arm and pulls Tamara close on his right. She is a little too heavy to carry, as well. They laugh, as he has no arms left for Sophia. So she hugs him close on Tamara's side. Paul acknowledges Mademoiselle's good wishes.

They walk pensively back, pulling each other close. Alexander, who lives in the same block, walks with them, practising his French quite competently with Mademoiselle, her commiserations and felicitations in French somehow sounding more sincere and effective than those made in Russian. The other two friends go, chatting quietly, to Block ten, further down the road towards the harbour. There is an uncomfortable mix of emotions, relief, even elation, at having avoided death but a sombre realisation that the danger has not yet entirely vanished.

They enter the apartment block's central archway and go through the first of the two doors on the right. The lift takes them all, squeezed in tight, to their floor. They relax, into the soft seats of the warm lounge and just gaze at one another, smiling weakly with relief.

Sophia wonders. Why does her happy and contented family have to suffer in this way? Paul is a good husband, a modern one. He treats her equally. They share their interest in books, music, art and nature. They are mostly in the same clubs, although Paul has his own hunting and business clubs and is a founder member of the Odessa Car Club. He volunteers with Society for the Care of Orphans. They have many Russian and international friends from the business, regional administration and consular communities and interact in Russian, German and French. For his degree studies, Paul also worked hard on his English. They have an extensive library of books in all four languages and travel widely. Their first, Tamara, was born in Hamburg. It is an exciting and fulfilling life.

They love their two girls equally. Tamara, the older, is so like Paul, in both looks and character. She is fair and will always be taller than Isa. She is the more serious and thoughtful one. Isa, like herself, is dark and also rounder, more spontaneous and possibly slightly naughtier. No, more mischievous. Most of the time, the two get on surprisingly well together. There is an almost conspiratorial allegiance between the two that Sophia loves.

***

A few days after the life-threatening experience with the red-haired Bolshevik, Paul's lawyer friend, Vadim, catches up with him in the street. He hooks his arm into Paul's.

'Pavel, you must help me find and expose that vicious Bolshevik to the authorities. He is dangerous.'

'I agree, he is very dangerous, Vadim but I'm sorry, I just can't help. I must concentrate on finding a way to get my family out of Odessa.'

Vadim does not manage to hunt down the Bolshevik before the Red Army is back, exactly as he had threatened. Only two months after the Park incident Paul and Sophia hear shooting and commotion in the night and the next morning, from his favourite balcony viewpoint, Paul sees that Marazlievskaya, and even some trees in their beautiful Park, are already hung with red banners. He breaks the terrible news to Sophia, who gasps and clasps her hands to her mouth.

The whole of the 'good' population that is not the Reds, again live in fear. They know that the plundering, nightly arrests and mass murder in the CheKa headquarters will start again. The first action the Bolsheviks take when occupying a town is to free the criminals and murderers. In Odessa, these will storm into the city, from the prison to the south and lead in the robbing and assassination of the Bourgeoisie. When the Bolshevik victors of Moscow and Petrograd arrived in Odessa, they declared the celebration of *Paradise on Earth*. For this, a notorious thief and murderer was promoted as a hero in the Odessa Grand Opera House. His chains were cut on stage with large bolt croppers - an allegory of the freeing of the people from the slavery of the Tsar - to the cheers of the watching rabble. These then swarmed out of the Opera and ransacked the more affluent areas of the city, stealing and destroying as they went.

Chapter 5 – Eviction

Tamara tells – in the nursery

'*Frère Jacques, Frère Jacques,*' sings my little sister and, as she continues with '*Dormez-Vous? Dormez-Vous?*' I join in to be followed finally by our governess. We, at last, manage to get into the swing of our roundelay. This, after two failed attempts, that had both ended in laughter. Mama appears at the nursery door.

She doesn't come in, says, '*Excusez-moi, Mademoiselle Voutaz*' and beckons with her finger.

'*S'il vous plaît continuer avec la pratique d'écriture que nous avons commencé hier,*' Mademoiselle instructs, as she joins Mama.

Isa gives me a look. I too am puzzled. It is very unusual for Mama to disturb our lessons. However, we guess it has to do with the nasty Bolsheviks taking over Odessa. We know that is why Mama has dressed as a peasant. We too have hidden our best dresses and now put on old, shabby clothes when we cross the road with Mademoiselle to stroll in Alexander Park. It is no longer safe to walk the streets of the town in smart clothing.

As Mama and Mademoiselle go to leave the room, there is Papa. He and Mama exchange a few quiet words in German, which means we are not supposed to hear. We understand bits, but of our three languages, it is the worst. Only Oma, Mama's mother insists on German. We are frightened. Mama has explained that the CheKa is almost certainly searching for our family and especially for Papa. Just because he is a business-man and a land-owner they call him a bourgeois bloodsucker and assume he is a supporter of the Tsarist White forces. If they find him, they will take him away for questioning. They have already dragged away some of Papa's close Russian business friends. Mama thinks it will not take long for the CheKa to discover where we live and then, some night, come banging on our door.

Papa comes into the nursery with a serious but kind face, crosses to the toy box and sits down. There is a little smile as he holds on to the lid and bounces gently up and down on the too many soft toys stuffed inside, but his serious face quickly returns. Papa and Mama have decided that we must try to escape to the German colony village of Grossliebental, outside Odessa, where Oma owns a house and where the Whites are still in control. Mademoiselle will not be coming and, when he sees our sad faces, he explains it would not be fair to put her through the danger.

***

Before Paul and Sophie can work out how they can escape from the threat they are facing in Odessa, they are forced to leave their apartment without warning. Paul returns from yet another fruitless shopping trip into town, where there is almost nothing to buy and what there is has to be queued for, to find the Red Army militia standing guard outside his apartment block. Fellow flat owners are milling around, angry and frightened at the same time.

The distraught block owner, Maria Anisimvona, rushes forwards and grabs him with both hands.

'Mr Vaatz, Mr Vaatz, this is terrible, unbelievable. The Red Army has stolen my property to use as their headquarters. Look at that awful sign they've put up. We are not allowed to remove anything, nothing at all. They've taken the whole block. What can we do?'

Paul looks up. A large, hand-written sign, red capitals on a grey–white canvas has been hung from balcony to balcony on the second floor. It declares, *Red Army Number 1 Headquarters.* It is completed with a bold red star. He is shattered. She is wide-eyed, hysterical and almost in tears. He can think of nothing helpful to say and mumbles that he will see what he can do. His position is slightly different, and this might just make it possible for him to save his belongings, if not his apartment. He decides to try the tactic he has shared with Sophia.

Thinking of Sophia reminds him. 'Where is she?' He does not need to look far. She is standing defiantly on the opposite side of the entrance arch to the armed guard, directly under the square enamelled number-plate, 14b, white on blue. With her are Tamara, Isa, the governess and the two loyal resident maids, each with a little bundle. Sitting there also is Max the Dachshund, well behaved and observing with intent interest the activity around him.

Paul confronts the Red commissar. 'This is not good enough! I must warn you; you have no right to confiscate my personal property. As a good Bolshevik, you will know of the great peace treaty signed between the German and Red armies. It's therefore obvious that you must allow me, as a German, to remove my effects.'

He senses that the commissar is disconcerted by this logic and cannot risk the disapproval of his superiors by refusing. It is also clear he is not at all keen to allow Paul to remove his belongings. Paul suspects the commissar has already set his mind on certain items that he could requisition for the state (and himself.) So after a pause, he sets Paul the condition that he must provide, firstly, a formal German Protest Certificate from the Swedish consulate (which is representing German interests in Russia) and secondly, an official pass for his effects from the newly established Bolshevik Accommodation Authority. The commissar hopes he has set Paul an impossible task, in the current chaotic administrative state of Odessa. Paul, however, is reasonably optimistic, as the Swedish Consul is a personal friend, and he calculates that Bolshevik officials at the Accommodation Authority are also likely to be sensitive to the peace treaty recently signed by their revered leader, Lenin.

Paul insists, before leaving on his crucial errand, that his family be allowed to return to their flat until the issue is resolved. There is the threat in his voice that if the commissar refuses, his superiors will be informed. The commissar begrudgingly instructs the guard to allow the family in. The noise level rises, as other flat owners question and complain, why they are not also allowed in? With his family safely back in their apartment, Paul hurries to Kanatnaya Street, 22 which runs parallel to Marazlievskaya, and is where the Swedish consulate is located.

As he goes, he ponders, poor Marazlievskaya; what would the Marazlis, father and son, have made of these awful happenings? Their initiative and investment, in the mid-eighteen-hundreds, had turned a derelict gunpowder magazine[5], located in rough wasteland on the edge of Odessa, into a beautiful park and a street of luxurious dwellings. The Bolsheviks are now calling Marazlievskaya, Engels Street. Engels, another German who, together with Marx, are the curse of Russia and for both of whom, that stupid England provided refuge instead of locking them up. And Ekaterininskaya is supposed to become Karl Marx Street? How will it all end?

Consul Oscar Osberg is an old Odessa Hunting Club friend and receives him warmly, at the same time lamenting how terrible the situation is. It is welcomingly peaceful and normal in his office compared to the chaos outside. Paul admires the impressive pair of trophy antlers that he remembers his friend bagging on a shoot they had been on together. They also reminisce of the challenges and excitement of the founding the Automobile Club and how they had treated the ladies to a drive and a picnic on the beach at Lustdorf.

---

[5] An ammunition store surrounded by earthen safety walls and situated in open space in case of explosion.

Ladies' day at the Odessa Automobile Club. Paul is standing second right at the back. Sophia sits third right in front. She looks rather serious. Her hat has flaps to pull down over her ears against the wind, when in the car.

The Consul organises for the German Protest Certificate to be quickly prepared and wishes Paul good luck as he hands it over. He proposes a toast to a better future with a Swedish Akvavit. It is very tempting to stay and talk longer as both friends silently and sadly realise that it is unlikely they will ever see each other again. But there is urgent business to complete, so they say earnest, heartfelt 'Goodbyes,' and Paul enters the streets towards his next challenge.

He loves his town with its wide, tree-shaded boulevards, giving a glimpse of the sea every now and again. Four and five-storey blocks line the streets through which he walks. The apartment blocks are solidly built of stone. Each has a generous arch through which a horse and carriage can drive into the yard at the centre. Some courtyards are simple, practical cobbled enclosures but others are hidden gems of tranquillity with fountains, statues and cared-for flower borders. The resident entrances, with their variously named letterboxes, are inside the arches on both the right and left. Beyond the arches, service doors open into the courtyards. This back entrance is known as the *chernaya dver*, or black door, in Russia. Each apartment block has its own architecture and stone colouring. The tiling of the broad pavement matches that of the block so, as one walks, the feet also experience a continuous change of scenery. The sellers, from the country, of boiled or roasted sweet corn or red-centred watermelon slices, no longer stand behind their carts at the street corners. Paul dreams of this past city atmosphere, as he hastens through the once smart streets, despairing of its future.

Although in a hurry he diverts a little to see what has happened in Deribasovskaya. He passes the Fabergé shop at number thirty-three. While smart, it is rather small and modest when one considers the fame of the name. It too has had its entrance broken in. Paul suspects, however, that most of the valuables were removed before the mob arrived. He had on exceptional occasions bought small items for Sophia, and he recalls how his mother had passed on to them when his father had died, a fabulous, solid-silver fish-serving set with not only the obligatory hall-mark but with 'Fabergé' written in large cursive script along the blade of its serving knife.

Near naked, writhing, oversized stone figures adorn many of the 19th-century buildings in this part of town. In the glass-covered

Passage, that cuts the corner of Deribasovskaya and Preobrashenskaya, they are particularly striking, with Herculean white marble effigies preventing the ornate balconies from falling to the pavement. These Hercules are paired with stone maidens of almost equal proportions, also quite capable of supporting a gallery or architrave. Other maidens empty bountiful cornucopias of fruit or heft sheaves of ripened wheat. All are accompanied by chubby winged cherubs. These Bourgeois symbols of happiness and plenty, being well above head level, have survived the looting, defacing and destruction and to Paul seem to be viewing the events happening below with a stony sadness.

Paul arrives at the Bolshevik Accommodations Authority in Grecheskaya Square, where the Reds have requisitioned a prestigious office block for their work. He is appalled to find yet another sad, angry, confused, milling crowd and a long, disorganised queue of people fighting and shouting to get in. It is evident that, if he queues, he will not get to see anyone that day. He searches for another way in and, through the archway, he locates the back, or 'black,' tradesmen's entrance. Here, as he had expected, a sturdy porter, with the red band of a revolutionary on his left arm, stops him. He is brusque and officious and makes it clear that Paul must enter by the main entrance. Paul, in response, is very polite and flattering. He explains that his business is most urgent and offers a silver Rouble. This is too tempting a bribe.

With a worried look on his face and concern in his voice, the porter allows him through on the strict promise that he tells no one.

'Otherwise,' he says, 'It will be me for the CheKa rather than you. Go to the far side of the yard and through that little door down two steps on the left.'

Paul follows the instructions. He walks purposefully through the door shutting it firmly but quietly behind him. The big hall is a bustle of busy, excited Bolshevik officials running around with papers and boxes and in earnest conversation. He is not noticed. The room stinks of wet leather, sweat and garlic. *Filthy, smelling, robbing, murdering Bolsheviks,* he thinks and picks out someone standing in the centre who appears to be directing affairs, and explains his business.

Without receiving a reply beyond, 'Follow me,' he is escorted to a large desk. On it are set out a thick open ledger, an inkstand with pen together with a stamp and inkpad. Behind sits a self-important looking commissar with the requisite red band around his right arm, a red star on his collar and, although indoors, still wearing his flat cap also decorated with a red star. He gives Paul a stern and unsympathetic look, ready to say 'No,' to whatever the request.

Paul is not intimidated by the aggressive look. He doesn't wait to be questioned but slams his German army demob papers, followed by the newly acquired German Protest Certificate, one after the other, on to the desk.

'This is a disgrace. Here am I a simple demobbed German Army soldier and your ignorant commissar in town is threatening to steal my belongings. Are you all so stupid that you forget the peace that has been signed between our two great armies? Just give me the authorisation document I need to recover my belongings.'

Nearby comrades look round to see what the noise is. The two officials are shocked and embarrassed by the outburst. They look at each other. After a pause, the one next to Paul, leans forward, places his hands, knuckles down, on the desk and says quietly to the other, 'I suggest we must issue the required documentation to this comrade soldier.'

The paper, signed by both officials and with a stamp in red ink that incorporates the Bolshevik star, is handed over. Paul is quietly triumphant. These stupid Bolsheviks, he thinks. They should have known that my address on Alexander Park is one of the most expensive in Odessa and that all town officials know me as a large landowner and businessman. They're probably peasants from the North who can hardly even read.

On the way out, Paul gives the worried porter a second tip and hopes sincerely; he will not suffer for letting him through.

Paul tells – Army papers

It was pure good luck to have those *Deutsches Herr* (German Army) demob papers to present to the commissars, showing me as a simple soldier. I was issued these when the German Army overran Odessa in

1918 and I, along with two of my cousins, offered our services as interpreters. As we had no military training, we were accepted but with the rank of musketeer, or simple private soldier. In retrospect, this low rank was a significant advantage when presenting my papers to the Bolshevik commissars. Later, when the German army was forced to leave Odessa, we requested our demob to allow us to remain with our families. However, to obtain those papers we had to go a long way back west to the West-Prussian Infantry regimental headquarters in Graudenz, West Prussia.

***

Paul dashes back to the apartment with his precious documents and presents them to the commissar who is still angrily fending off the pleas and questions of the other poor flat owners. He is not at all pleased to see Paul and even less his papers, but he can tell they are authentic.

At once, he sets another challenging hurdle. 'Alright, I see this authorises you to take your stuff, but you must be out by mid-day tomorrow and what you do not remove by then will become the property of the people.'

He smirks as he thinks that this time he has set an impossible task, this owner has to empty his expensively furnished eight-room flat on the second floor in just six hours. Paul ignores the smirk; his mood and energy are now high. He is determined to achieve this task within the time given. All that night the family and the servants pack and prepare.

Pleas from fellow flat dwellers for Paul to smuggle precious items out for them complicate the removal of the family's effects. To try and perform this favour is dangerous for if discovered, would almost certainly lead to him being shot. The attitude of the commissar and his Red Guards is openly hostile, and they would welcome any excuse to sabotage the evacuation.

That night Paul's is the only family in the whole block. The building sounds and feels as it is; sad and empty. It echoes. Several flat doors have been broken-down and stand open. These will have been the apartments where the owners were absent when the Red

Militia arrived. Paul doubts that any residents would have refused the Reds entry. To have done so would have been fatal. The complete belongings of those owning the flats remain there. Those who were in when the military arrived now have only the clothing they were wearing plus the few things they were allowed to carry out. Those who were not in are even worse off.

It seems that Paul will manage to rescue his most essential belongings, but he is still depressed. He feels for his fellow flat owners who have lost practically everything they owned. These are friends many are close friends. Even the quirky and not so companionable do not deserve this treatment. And there is nothing he can do to help or minimise their distress. He does manage to recover some small items for four friends living in flats close to his own. Three requests are for jewellery that Paul has to extract from secret hiding places; one of these is from a young Jewish family, living on the floor above. The fourth favour is for his old friend, Alexander. It is for some photographs and a leather-bound family Bible, with a clasp. The Bible is rather heavy, and Paul suspects it also conceals precious jewellery, but he does not pry. He is only able to fulfil these requests because the guards are kept outside. Only the commissar and his second-in-command occasionally patrol the interior stairways and corridors. They do explore the apartments, and no doubt, steal items for themselves.

As soon as Paul returns from his altercations with the commissar, the family, maids and Mademoiselle start to pack. They must make difficult decisions as to what to keep and what to leave. Much clothing and most of the toys fail the 'essential' test. The two loyal live-in maids receive presents that they at first try to refuse but accept when Sophia explains, it's either them or the Bolsheviks. Paul and Sophia realise that the maids are in danger of being harassed as suspected sympathisers of their bourgeois masters, so it is agreed that they should leave early in the evening, before dark. They will need to make it clear to the guards outside that they have no such sympathy. The two have friends in town with whom they can stay until they are able to return to their villages.

The packing continues through much of the night. China and glass are wrapped in newspaper and protected further with the clothes they decide to keep. All are placed in a variety travelling trunks and suitcases. Sophia and Mademoiselle undertake this task assisted by the girls. Sophia has decided it is better to allow Tamara and Isa to stay up and help with packing than to try to get them to sleep with activity and excitement all around. Her strategy works, they manage to stay awake, and are truly helpful, until almost midnight and then ask to go to bed – a unique request from them.

The grown-ups finish their task soon after. As Paul gets ready to turn off the light before they go to sleep, he acknowledges to Sophia that, while he would have insisted that the girls go to bed at their proper time, her strategy distracted from them worrying about what the future holds.

Next morning at six, as the two horse-drawn low-loaders position themselves below the windows of his flat, Paul notices the Red Guards giving them meaningful looks and muttering to each other. He suspects this is because the Red Army has requisitioned almost all horses and wagons and the guards are wondering from where and how he had managed to obtain them. Only massive bribery achieved this miracle. More silver roubles encourage the removers to work quickly. Soft goods such as duvets, linen and clothes are just thrown over the balconies directly on to the wagons. Even the heavy furniture is removed, including bookcases, a large buffet and the mahogany Bernstein grand piano. There is much grunting and contradictory instructions given as to how best to navigate the corners. There are boxes and boxes of Paul's beloved books. The china and glass boxes were to have been brought down by the electric lift. However, the electricity is off, so these also need to be carted down. Current is restored, only in the last hour, at eleven, which makes bringing down the final pieces that little bit faster and easier.

While supervising the removal Paul and Sophia are disturbed to see that the armed Red Guards are not beyond inspecting what is being removed and demanding for themselves any odd bits and pieces they fancy. They engage in such thievery even though there is official approval for their removal. It is not easy to argue with a menacing, heavily armed guard. How to ensure the guards do not find the jewellery? Sophia quickly devises a scheme. The precious items had been carefully parcelled up the night before. Mademoiselle now lowers small packages from the kitchen window, in a shopping basket. Sophia is waiting in the courtyard below, where Paul keeps one of his Mercedes demonstration cars. She arranges the packages in the girls' two prams. The girls march out with them. The guard at the archway, a family man, puts his rifle aside as Isa passes and admires her doll.

'She's very pretty. What is her name?' and pats its head.

'Pupsi.'

'That's a lovely name,' He pats it on the head again and pretends to tuck it in properly.

Isa just looks at him and smiles, as she does not quite realise the importance of her mission. Tamara, behind, does and almost jumps forward to object but luckily stops herself when she sees that he does not intend to do a search. She then quickly strides past the guard giving him a sweet smile but no time to admire her carefully tucked in doll. Paul stands by the wagons, watching nervously as the prams emerge from the archway pushed by his two girls. Rescuing the jewellery and silver is essential, as Paul and Sophia know it is very likely that in the following weeks and months their barter could help to keep them alive. That car in the yard, Paul knows won't be his for much longer, and in any case, it would not be much use as petrol is now wholly unavailable to the ordinary person.

The massive evacuation is completed just in time, even though they have to leave behind some less essential items, including most of the children's toys. This is a little ironic as it is the doll's prams that enabled them to bring out their valuable items. The two prams are left behind, standing forlornly at the kerbside, only then to be curiously inspected by the Red guards. They will probably remain there unclaimed, as no Bolshevik will wish to be found in possession of such a bourgeois item.

Paul is lucky to hail a *droshky* (An open horse-drawn taxi) which stops. He tells Sophia, Mademoiselle and the girls to go ahead. Tamara has Maxi, the dog on her lap, but both girls are near to tears, as Papa has let, their canary, Twinkle free through the window, as they could not take him and it would be cruel to leave him to the

Bolsheviks. The girl's cat, Mitzi has just disappeared in the noise and confusion. Paul plans to follow Sophia to Mrs Van Dych's, a friendly old Dutch lady, born in Russia, like they, where he has managed to find a room in the north-western outskirts of Odessa. He will first make sure that all the goods are firmly stowed and then follow.

Chapter 6 – Marazlievskaya

Having seen the two heavily laden wagons depart safely, he prepares to leave his house in Marazlievskaya where his family has lived so happily for eleven years. He shouts for a droshky for himself. The few that remain in Odessa and that have not been destroyed, as symbols of the Bourgeoisie, are mostly no longer driven by their regular registered drivers. Enterprising revolutionaries have requisitioned them. In other cases, the original drivers will have stolen the droshkies from their former masters, more often than not after murdering them as bourgeois collaborators. Other revolutionaries get free passage and then race around the city shouting slogans and firing their guns, mostly in the air but sometimes carelessly killing an innocent passer-by. Real customers, such as Paul must pay an excessive rate. He finds it perverse that such so-called Communists are finding independent ways of earning and extorting money from others. So for the second time, Paul agrees to an unreasonable fare.

Marazievskya, 14b today. Paul and Sophia's Apartment block. The main difference between 1908, when they arrived, and today is the growth of the trees in an hundred years. Their apartment was on the 2nd floor.

As he is stepping into his droshky, he feels a tap on his shoulder and hears, 'Do you remember who I am?'

He turns slowly. Standing there is a strong young man of about twenty-five, a Bolshevik in revolutionary uniform with red bands across his chest and around his left arm, with a five-pointed red (what Paul sees as a) Jewish star on his cap and pointing the large pistol in his fist at Paul's stomach. Immediately he knows whom he is facing and shivers violently inside. It is the red-haired Bolshevik who tried to have him and his friends shot like vermin only two months ago. His new uniform with its red flashes shows he has risen in the Red hierarchy and is anxious to show his power. Paul is shattered after everything having gone so well. He decides to say nothing, shows surprise and pretends not to recognise his questioner.

'Then I will tell you,' the red-head continues, 'I am the one who told you that we Bolsheviks would return and hang you up like dogs. Now we have the power again, and we will sweep you away. You are the one I saw run into this door and at whom my comrades shot but missed. We can remedy that error now. Stand against the wall! I will order the guards there, to shoot you as a Bourgeois collaborator!'

Paul sees that only a block away there is a truck carrying CheKa militiamen who are preparing to enter, plunder and murder its owners. These can quickly be summoned to execute him. He stands as if in a dream. The shock overwhelms him. For a moment he feels nothing, hears nothing and nothing is important anymore. He is in a trance. He feels beyond rescue, as those who know the Bolsheviks are aware, these beasts in human form show no mercy, sympathy, fairness or conscience, in fact, any human feeling. As Paul hears the Bolshevik's words, he silently waves good-bye to this world.

He thinks of his dear, loyal Sophia, who has innocently just left and who will be waiting at Mrs Van Dych's, quietly but impatiently. He imagines her repeatedly looking at the small gold enamelled Borel Neuchatel watch he gave her for her last birthday. In his mind he sees his two girls playing with their dolls or perhaps taking lessons with their governess, which they should be doing at this time of day. Never again will he see them and hug them. How will Sophie learn what has happened to me? How will she survive? She will. She has initiative and will make sure the girls aren't harmed. But how they will cry. What a sorry world this is, how transitory, stupid, cruel and pointless everything is. Is this wretched, miserable mankind, determined to continue with its endless mutual murdering and tearing limb from limb, even as the beautiful sun continues to shine in the innocent blue heaven forever?

He opens his eyes and looks at that blue sky. He recalls how happy the sun had made him as a little boy on the farm in Schastlivka where he had been born. He remembers how he had lain on his back in the long grass, on the edge of the field in which the peasants were working. He had plucked a blade of grass and sucked at the sweetness at its base. He had shaded his eyes and watched the skylarks rising and singing and tried to judge whether it was really true that the higher they flew, the higher their note. Lying in the grass, he had heard the peasants singing as they worked and remembered how kind and friendly they always were.

As he waits to hear the voice of the Bolshevik summoning the militia to execute him, he becomes furious thinking how the Bolsheviks have turned these innocent, kindly people into savages. This anger gives him strength. To hell with the Bolsheviks! I have a family to save. I will not submit meekly to being shot. I will use my intelligence and flatter this bullying, ignorant upstart peasant to set me free. There is plenty of time to die. Perhaps I can use revolutionary arguments and play on this beast's wish to be seen as a hero. Perhaps I can engage him in a lengthy political debate.

What Paul fears most is that the Bolshevik will recognise him as the one who had asked where he had stolen the telescope. Nothing, he knows, offends these revolutionary heroes more than accusing them of what they are, that is thieves and murderers. For, in the name of the Revolution and of right and equality, they loot property to share among themselves. He then realises that the Bolshevik does not recognise him as the one who had accused him of stealing the telescope but has confused him with his dear friend Vadim, who had run away from the gunmen. This realisation reassures him that there might be a way out.

So he lowers his gaze from the sky, looks the Bolshevik straight in the eyes, places a right hand firmly on the other's shoulder, smiles and says in a somewhat theatrical voice,

'Comrade, I can see that you are a true leader of the Revolutionary Guard, and I assume that you support justice. You would not wish to compromise the revolutionary principles of freedom, equality and brotherliness by the murder of an innocent foreigner. I must tell you I am not the man you think I am, and I am not involved in your internal war. I am a German citizen and have papers to prove it. You will know of the peace that has been agreed between our two great governments, and you would not wish it to be said that you had broken that agreement. Finally, I am not the man who ran from you on that day in March.'

The Bolshevik shuffles awkwardly and smiles at the flattery. He stands there, self-conscious, happily earnest and good-natured. His angry frown vanishes and his expression changes from that of the beast it had been seconds before to that of a sturdy, friendly round-faced Russian peasant from the country which is what he would have been before this terrible civil war started.

'We Bolsheviks are the people's revolutionaries and no murderers. We are preparing the Russian people for a true paradise on Earth. Our dear, precious Mother Russia will soon be the happiest and freest land in the World. I fought in the Great War. I was a prisoner of war in Germany, I had to work deep underground, but I have also seen wonderful things. It was Germany who let our Great Leader Lenin come back to us, without him our glorious Revolution would not have happened! But how can you prove that you are not the person at whom my comrades were shooting? I saw you jump into the house that is just behind you.'

As Paul is worrying and wondering how he can answer this question, he realises that Dymtrus, the Ukrainian caretaker of Block 14b, who is standing close by, must have heard the whole conversation. In desperation, he asks the caretaker whether he had seen the shooting two months ago and whether he, Paul is the man who was running away.

Without any prompting the caretaker answers convincingly,

'Yes, yes I saw everything, and no, it cannot possibly have been you, sir. That man was much shorter and in any case, it was not this entrance but the next one up, in block sixteen, that he ran into.'

At this, the Bolshevik at once relaxes, makes an ironic little bow, and somewhat grandly waves Paul away with a sweep of his arm.

'All right, I believe you. I don't want the murder an innocent man on my conscience. Also, you are a foreigner. You can go.'

***

Paul rushes off to his family at Mrs Dych's apartment block. As he enters the room where they are still organising themselves, the girls run to greet him. He gives each a big kiss and asks what they have been doing. Apparently exploring the house, getting to know the other tenants, who spoil them, and searching for other children to play with, but not finding any. He shushes them off to play.

'What's happened?' His face and the fact that he got rid of the girls so quickly tells Sophia something is wrong. He puts his left arm around her shoulders and sits her down with himself.

'That Bolshevik almost had me shot, again.'

'No! Again? How .....?'

Paul describes the whole episode in detail, recalling, as he speaks, how close he had come to giving up, and how he could easily now be dead. Sophia understands this too. For a while, they sit, locked together with Sophia's head on Paul's shoulder. Sophia then straightens.

'You're alive, and I thank God for that. Let's check that everything has arrived safely.'

They go into the room where their boxes and furniture, from Marazlievskaya, have been somewhat randomly piled. They rearrange it in better order and reassure themselves that everything has been delivered. There is one exception. Paul gets angry when he discovers that his prize Belgian Frankott hunting rifle, bought while he was a student studying in Antwerp, has been stolen. He calms when Sophia reminds him that it is a small sacrifice to pay for securing the safety of the family.

They must get out of Odessa altogether, to one of the many long-established German villages in the countryside surrounding Odessa. He and Sophia have already decided to aim for Grossliebental where Sophia was born and where Oma, Sophia's mother, owns a house. She is now living with the tenants to whom she lets the house. Sophia had persuaded her to leave earlier-on when things started to get nasty. She had dressed as a village woman and experienced no problems in getting past the Red guards at the city boundaries.

The family's eviction from their apartment had been so sudden and unplanned that Mademoiselle had just accompanied them. But following Paul's second life-threatening experience, all agree that her long-term safety is not guaranteed. At present, someone carrying the papers of a neutral country is probably safe. But for how long will this last? All have noticed how the Reds are getting less and less bothered as to whom they harass, arrest and even murder. Paul and Sophia also realise it would not be fair to try and persuade her to come with them to the German villages, further away from Odessa.

Mademoiselle stays the night and is ready to set off early next morning. She should have no problem in getting passage from the harbour to a Black Sea port, further west, in Romania or Bulgaria, that will allow her to continue to Switzerland. The Reds, of course, will monitor and question anyone trying to leave but her papers, showing her as a teacher from Switzerland, should ensure she has no difficulties. Paul gives her six months pay, and Sophia and the girls wish her good luck. All are very sorry to see her leave and there are held-back tears as kisses and polite but very genuine goodbyes are exchanged in French. Paul offers to try and get a droshky, but she says it's probably safer to walk the three kilometres, looking like a humble peasant. All give a final wave as she turns left at the corner into Lyustdorfskaya Road that leads directly back to the centre of the city.

Chapter 7 – Deadly sailors

One evening as Paul returns to their temporary lodgings, he notices two sailors in their blue uniforms and square white striped flap collars, sitting outside the house. Their sailor hats are lying beside them on the bench, rifles casually stacked against the side of the house. They are sitting in the sun, eating sunflower seeds in the typical Russian peasant way. They stuff a handful of whole grains in their mouth, skilfully de-husk them using tongue and teeth and then spit out the husks, one by one, in a little pile on the ground. Each sailor already has his mound, building up nicely beside the leg on his side of the bench. They look relaxed and harmless. But Paul is immediately suspicious, as sailors are some of the most active and extreme revolutionaries and have committed atrocious crimes against their officers.

In Odessa harbour, after they mutinied in 1905, they pushed their officers into the ship's boiler fires, tied their hands and feet and threw them in the water or locked them in animal cages and starved, teased and taunted them.

When a diver was sent down to work early in 1918, no sooner was he at the bottom than he was signalling to be taken up again. He surfaced frightened and shivering, acting like a mad man and stuttered that he had been encircled by standing dead men. These will have been innocent officers who had had weights tied to their feet before being pushed overboard. The gases in their bodies had made them stand upright and the current to move them eerily in the water. It was the sailors of in the infamous gunship *Almaz*, moored in Odessa harbour who had perpetrated these gruesome atrocities.

The sailors, therefore, make Paul very uncomfortable, and he has to decide whether to enter the door or not. In reality, he has no option as his family is inside. So he walks in as casually as he can giving a short but polite greeting. The sailors do not look up, reply with a grunt and do not try to stop him.

Once in he asks his new Dutch friend why the sailors stand guard outside. She answers that they are caught as in a mousetrap. The sailors are letting everyone in but nobody out. Everyone in the house that holds several tenants is worried. Many have lived there for fifteen to twenty years and not only know but are friends with both other tenants and the owner. They come together and discuss what action the Bolsheviks are planning. It is evident that if no one is being let out that some sort of interrogation is intended, or that someone will be arrested and sent to the CheKa. And very few come out of the CheKa alive. Everyone gets tired late into the night and tries to sleep, but all are restless and cannot. At one in the morning, their landlady knocks gently on Paul's room door and advises the family to get dressed quickly as a troop of armed CheKa military has arrived and are interrogating one of her oldest tenants; old in age and old in length of stay. As it is likely they will carry out further interrogations, it is best to be dressed.

A young officer of Denikin's White army has the room next to Paul's family. He is busy burning incriminating papers and evidence, including his officer rank shoulder tabs. As an active officer of the Denikin army, he is in great danger; the Bolsheviks have a practice of literally taking the skin from the living body of their victims and cutting the Tsarist epaulette markings into the skin on their shoulders. Paul feels desperately sorry for the man, knocks on his room door and offers to help. He is very young, only about twenty-three, a strong blond boy with bright blue eyes and with a solemn, snow-white face. He has the look of an authentic Russian of noble blood. His movements are soft, his features refined but most noticeable are his hands. They are more like that of a girl than that of a Russian officer.

'I wish I could help you.' Paul offers. 'Do you have many more things to destroy? You must be quick. The CheKa can come any minute.'

'And then?' He replies. 'I will let them politely into my room, and if they find anything incriminating, I will shoot the bastards. I will not be taken to the CheKa. One dies one way or another. Better this way.'

And he pulls a Browning pistol out of his pocket.

Paul suggests that he should go out by the kitchen 'black' door into the dark yard and try and hide until the Reds have gone.

'If you are discovered in the yard which is very unlikely then you can still have the pleasure of shooting down the Reds.'

'It is not as simple as you suggest.' He answers. 'I know that when the Red bastards visit a building, they guard the back door just like the front. I would rather remain in the comfort of my room and wait than to be cold and lonely in the yard.'

Paul stays a while longer, talking. Sophia also comes and sits with them as they wait for the CheKa's next move.

Mrs Van Dych knocks, comes quietly into the room, and informs them that it is all over and is now safe. The CheKa has gone. But by her sad face, they can tell that there is also bad news. After a long, painful interview, her longest residing resident, and good friend has been hauled away to the CheKa. The crime of this unlucky man is merely to be an official of the local government in Odessa. That is sufficient to label him as a counter-revolutionary. A consolation is that the young White Army officer is safe for now. So ends a miserable and upsetting night with the household going to bed for the second time at three in the morning.

***

Their landlady tells them that the 'Day of the Poor' had been declared in Odessa, two days before. This Bolshevik proclamation authorised every proletarian, every beggar, anyone who thought they had the right, to go from the street into any rich or other house and to take any items they wished that they consider indispensable to them. Paul lists this event as yet another Bolshevik trick firstly, to legitimise the stealing from the rich and wealthy by the poorer and lower levels of society; secondly, to win the support of the proletariat to the Red cause; thirdly, to set the two classes on a life and death war against each other; and lastly to arouse, in the more impoverished masses (90% of the population,) a utopian vision of paradise on Earth and of Mother Russia.

The worst atrocities occurred in the best and wealthiest quarters of the city, but the crazed mob did not limit itself to these, it also looted middle-class homes and committed murder and rape there.

Paul sees now how lucky he has been that the Bolsheviks threw him out of his apartment with his belongings just two days ago. They could hardly have done him a greater favour. The family is lucky too that the riots have not yet spread to the outskirts where they are staying. He must get his family right out of the city and to the German colony villages as soon as he can.

Chapter 8 – Bolshevik Guard Post

A few days later a young farmer from Grossliebental arrives with a message from Oma that she has found a wagon and that Sophia's cousin Wilhelm would come early next morning to bring them to the village. The thirty versts (1 Verst = 1.07km) cart-drive will take most of the day, so they boil the sweet corn that Oma has sent with the messenger and pack it for the journey. There is also a little salt which has become very rare and precious since the Revolution started. Sophia fills two milk cans with water. Then she sends the girls to bed, but they chat with excitement.

Paul's official citizen pass contains damning words such as landowner and business-man. He considers himself cursed three times, as bloodsucker, White sympathiser and counter-revolutionary and stays up trying to work out a strategy to get himself past the Red guard posts. He also worries for the family for if he is caught, they would be tarred with the Bourgeois brush and treated accordingly. In the end, he has to give up and sleeps fitfully nestled close to his beloved Sophie. Next morning they are all up and ready when cousin Wilhelm arrives at seven.

Tamara tells

Mama's cousin, Wilhelm, who has volunteered to drive the cart, arrives early. He has brought a simple un-sprung farmer's wagon rather than a smart phaeton or droshky. This is so that the Red guards will assume we are simple farmers taking goods back to our village. Papa frowns when Wilhelm mentions he has noticed several guard-posts at the city borders. Wilhelm reassures Papa he will leave the city by a back road where there is unlikely to be a guard-post.

We help to load the cart with the food we got ready last evening, plus essential clothing and other things we will need in Grossliebental. We are each allowed a toy. I decide on my favourite German Marienfeld china-faced doll, which Mama says is silly, as it is bound to get broken, but she still allows me to take it. I also have charge of Maxi who finds all the preparations very exciting. He knows he is going on a journey. Isa takes her little grey, Steif kitten. Before today the kitten didn't have a name but she now is calling it Mitzi in memory of our lost cat. We all dress as peasants. Although the situation is dangerous, I can't help giving Isa a nudge and making her laugh at Papa, who looks so uncomfortable and funny in the dirty old worker's flat-cap that he has on. As part of his disguise, he has no collar and has taken off the gold-rimmed glasses he always wears. So now he can't see well, and this makes him appear confused. Mama, however, looks like a contented peasant in her shawl and headscarf. Papa worries that the two well-fed black horses that Wilhelm has managed to keep from the Bolsheviks might give us away as bourgeois. Wilhelm simply shrugs and says there is nothing he can do.

We are only halfway along Franzuskiyi Boulevard, on our way to the town boundary, when a band of drunken revolutionaries in a stolen droshky comes charging along the street towards us. They are bawling revolutionary songs and shooting their rifles, mostly into the air, but some shots hit the buildings and could kill innocent pedestrians. A long queue stands outside a boarded-up shop, hoping to buy something to eat. They shrink to the ground and scramble into doorways to avoid the stray bullets. Maxi barks and tries to get out of my hold to see what is happening but I hold him tight. I am frightened those nasty Reds might try and shoot him. We make ourselves as small as we can, but the noisy gang sweeps harmlessly by as Wilhelm shouts a comradely greeting and gives them a friendly wave of his whip.

We can tell there has been fighting and looting. There are bullet holes in the walls. The smart shops have shattered windows with a mess inside and with rejected booty, that looters have decided was too heavy or they could not after all use, left scattered on the pavements. The damage gets less as we move further out of town, but Papa becomes more nervous, and Wilhelm sits more erect and alert, his eyes searching the road ahead. The horses strain to pull our cart up a long slope and then the way plunges steeply down again.

There, half-way down, is a guard post. We all look at Wilhelm.

Papa, sitting together with him in front, gives him a stare that says, Well, what do we do now? Mama is perched on a large trunk with her back towards Papa. We are on the floor of the cart at her knees. She reaches behind to hold and squeeze Papa's hand and gives us a smile and what is meant to be an encouraging little nod. Wilhelm does not seem concerned. He mumbles something about having a plan but does not explain, which I can tell makes Papa even more fidgety. Isa and I hug each other and cannot decide whether to be frightened or excited.

Now Wilhelm does something peculiar. He edges the cart forward so that it is in full view of the guards. Next, he hands the reins to Papa and gets down to the horses. Papa and Mama are clearly wondering why he is wasting time adjusting the horse tackle as if there is something wrong. Wilhelm spends a few minutes at this, moving from one horse to the other and making sure that the guards are watching.

He cups his hands and shouts down, 'Comrades, have you got a leather strap or some rope? Our horse trappings are torn, and I worry the cart might not be able to stop on this steep hill.'

After a short pause, one shouts back that he is sorry but that they have nothing and cannot help.

Wilhelm climbs back up into the driving seat and, as he takes back the reins and settles himself, says to Papa, 'Right! Hold tight. We're going down as fast as we can as if our brakes are gone. You *pretend* to pull the brake, hard.'

He then urges his two horses downwards, faster and faster while leaning back and acting as if he was trying to slow them. Horses and cart career down the hill, bouncing and shaking on the rough road and gathering speed, straight towards the post. We two are lifted off the boards by the bumpy ride and are holding onto and peeping over the side. Mama tries to push our heads down and is telling us to hide. A water-can falls over onto my feet. Maxi has wriggled out of my hold and is standing, with front paws on the tailboard, barking furiously. Papa, with his lips held together in determination, does as he is told and grips the brake lever firmly with both hands, but I can tell he is not pulling at all.

'Sorry comrades, I can't stop the horses,' Wilhelm yells as the cart charges past the startled guards.

I don't know who is more surprised, the guards or we. Papa says afterwards that his main worry had been that the two guards would shoot. But I saw how they jumped back and made room, watching open-mouthed, wide-eyed and with their weapons held sideways out of the way.

Still in sight of the guard-post but far enough away to feel safe, Wilhelm makes a big show of stopping the horses, with loud shouts of, 'Whoa' and an exaggerated pulling back of the reins. Maxi jumps out and runs round and round the carriage barking furiously. Luckily the horses come from a farm and are used to such noise and look down at him with distain. Wilhelm gets down, pretends to readjust the tackle, and while doing this, he turns and shouts apologies to the guards. They wave back and wish our family a safe journey.

Papa is impressed and hugs Wilhelm close, patting him hard on the back. Mama also envelops him and gives him three kisses - left, right, left. Isa says to me that that was the best carriage ride she has ever had, much more exciting than trip, trap tripping to an afternoon children's performance at the Grand Opera House, in a boring old droshky with Mademoiselle. So, with this latest danger behind us, we trot off happily towards Grossliebental where we hope to be safe.

Half-way on our journey, we pass through the village of Tatarka. Mama and Papa joke about a strange man from Tatarka who had talked to them in Ekaterininskaya Square, asking where he could buy bread, when they were watching the Bolshevik May Day celebrations. They say I would not understand the joke.

It is a relief to arrive safely in Grossliebental and at Oma's house at number nine Steinstrasse. We are bubbling over to tell her the story of our down-hill dash past the guards.

She exclaims, *'Boshe Moi,'* ('My God!') holds her hands high in the air and then places them both on her cheeks in amazement, and praises God for our safe arrival. Then the grown-ups talk sleeping arrangements. The tenants in her house have already made room for Oma. The problem is there is not room for us all, as the tenants also have children. Papa and Mama agree that they will stay with Oma and that we should sleep two doors away with Anya, a distant cousin. At first, I am not sure about the arrangement, and Isa starts whining, if not quite crying. But Anya comes over to welcome us and is very warm and friendly and shows us our room with a doll's house and other toys belonging to her now grown-up daughter. So we accept and are happy to call her 'Aunty.'

Tamara, Isa and Linke cousins in Grossliebental in happier times.

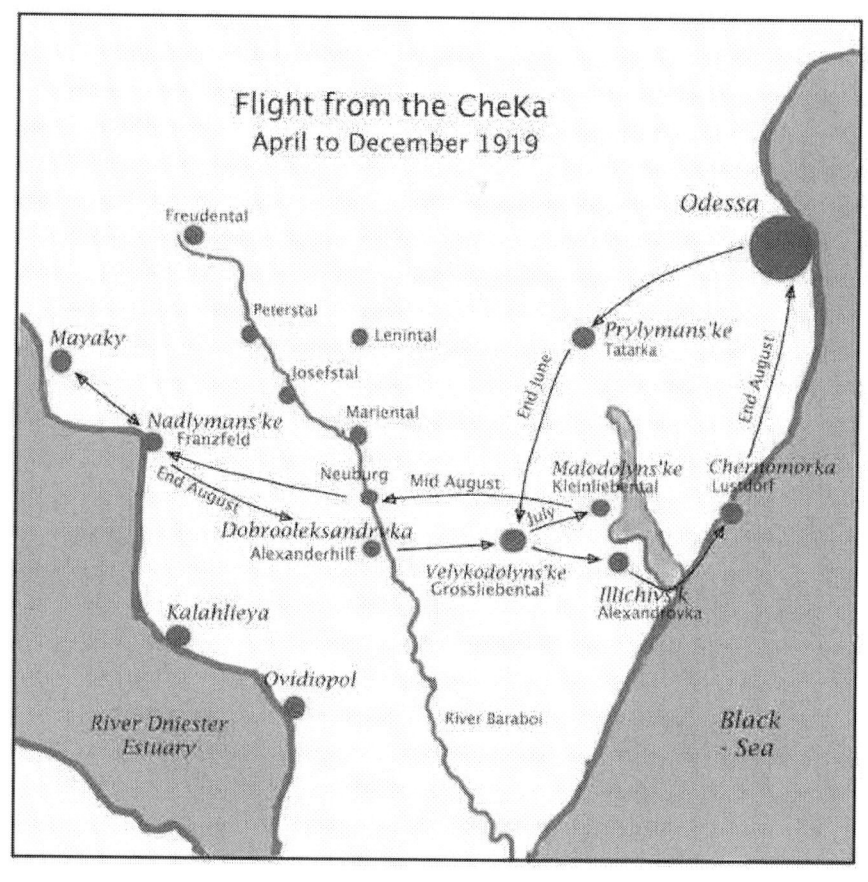

Running from the CheKa – the flight path

Chapter 9 – Grossliebental Cemetery

Tamara and Isa wake up next morning and explore the village before breakfast. Oma's house is very close to the village square with its solid church built of the local limestone, on one side. There is also a schoolhouse and a community centre in a similar style. The villagers' houses are all alike. They are single-story, long and narrow and have a pitched roof, thatched with reeds. Cellars have been cut into the limestone on which the village lies with the stone being used for the house walls. The rear of the house is for the animals; mainly chickens, donkeys and goats, but also the odd horse or cow. Most of these bigger animals are housed in barns at the edge of the village. Each house has an ample garden, all round and so they are quite widely spaced. Each invariably has a tended vegetable plot. Some villagers also show off their flowers, while others seem to think them a waste of time. The cellars are used for storage, mainly to keep food fresh in summer and to protect it from frost in winter. Dried animal manure is still used as a fuel for heating, but the colonists have now planted copses of trees, on the previously bare Steppe-land, and systematically harvest these for firewood.

At breakfast, for which the girls go across to Oma Kundert's house, Mama suggests a visit to the village cemetery one verst to the south. She wants to share one of her happiest childhood memories. They walk hand-in-hand across the square from the house past the *Konsum* or village shop on the left into the narrow School Street, and then also on the left, a row of village institutions; the administration, the waifs' home, the central school, the village church, the pastor's house and the poor home, then through the new graveyard and along the straight avenue of overhanging mulberry trees. Finally they cross the railway line that skirts the village. Maxi follows obediently behind. He does not need to be on the lead. On the other side of the line, a gate in the willow hedge leads into the cemetery. There Mama points out the headstones belonging to founder family members of the colony. These had arrived in Russia during the reign of Tsar Alexander I in 1805. This, however, is not her main reason for bringing the girls here.

Close to the cemetery entrance is a small but steep hillock. Maxi, even with his short legs is first and looks down at them wagging his tail, as if wondering why these humans are so slow. Mama follows with the girls and at the top takes a deep breath. She then slowly turns on the spot absorbing the view. Next, she gathers Tamara and Isa, each under one arm and rotates together with them towards the Black Sea. She names, in order, all the bays and estuaries they can see stretching from the horizon towards them. Far away on the coast are the gold church domes of their Odessa, sparkling in the sun, from which they had escaped only two days before. Closer to them, on the Suchoi estuary, is the small Catholic village of Kleinliebental with its lighthouse. As she turns with them to the left and puts the sea behind, there is the Greek colony village of Alexandrovka. They swivel further, and she points out the battlements of the old fort of Ackermann silhouetted on the horizon on the other side of the broad River Dniester estuary. She explains that the Ottoman Turks built it long ago when they ruled the coast.

Having shown them her favourite view, Sophia takes a last look round and starts down again. The girls decide to race. Isa, of course, falls over her feet halfway down and rolls the rest of the way. She sits up quickly, which is good as Sophia has already let out a cry that stops short when she hears Isa laughing, as Maxi jumps all over her trying to lick her face. At the railway line, Tamara and Isa wait and watch Sophia come down, holding her skirts like a lady, although still dressed as a peasant in her shawl. Isa is given a little slap at the back of the head and,

'You be more careful, young lady, you could have hurt yourself.'

Plat map of Großliebental
Source: *Erinnerungen an die deutschen Kolonien des Großliebentaler Rayons bei Odessa*
Map courtesy of the Black Sea German Research plat map collection
This map also appears in *Homesteaders on the Steppe*, p. 332-333

Grossliebental – visit to the old cemetery from Oma Kundert's house

At Sophia's suggestion, they take a longer route back, follow the railway to the east and then turn left along the main road back into the village. A train rattles past, enveloping them in steam and smoke. The girls end up coughing and laughing at the same time. The driver blows the piercing engine whistle and waves. The girls wave back. The train is packed with soldiers, and they exchange waves with them also.

That is fun until Sophia recovers from the smoke and the noise and says quietly, 'Those were Red Army soldiers. They had red flashes on their hats and sleeves.'

She tells Papa when they return to the house together, and he looks concerned. Only days later, Bolshevik requisitioning parties start to visit Grossliebental and the surrounding villages to demand hay, grain and horses. They expect to receive these supplies without payment.

'In support of the Party,' They say.

As the demands grow, so the villagers become increasingly angry at this confiscation of their produce and wealth. Sophia explains to the girls that a war council has been formed, including the headmen from nearby villages and White Army officers who are hiding in the community. Paul also volunteers. The council of villages has agreed that they will retaliate if the requisitioning demands become too extreme.

Chapter 10 – Grossliebental Murder

It is 20th July. Tamara and Isa are playing in the sparse grass in front of the house on the village square when an open truck appears carrying militia in black uniforms. The men jump out. Three go to the community hall, bang on the door and are let in. The rest stand in little groups looking disdainful and in charge as if they owned the village. They light cigarettes, unsling their rifles and lean them and themselves against the truck. Two of the village elders come seeking additional committee members. One of these is Paul, and he goes to join them. It is the committee that Johann Kundert, Paul's father-in-law, would have chaired as the colony villages head, had he survived the cholera epidemic of 1899. There is an unreal quiet in the square in which one hears animal noises not noticed before. The women and the older men who are not working, wait.

Inside the community hall, the three uninvited visitors sit staring across a trestle table at the ten members of the villages committee. In addition to the Russian commissar, who it appears comes from Petersburg, Paul is surprised to find that one, Schmitt, is a German sailor and the other, Syrik, an Austrian soldier, both must be Spartakists (German communists, possibly freed prisoners of war.) He despises them as traitors. The two German speakers appear to take a perverse pleasure in presenting their excessive demands. These are for one million in paper roubles, one hundred thousand in gold roubles, twenty horses, thirty cattle plus forty young village men for the Red Army. It is this last demand, for young villagers to join the Red Army, which especially enrages the committee. They flatly reject it and refuse to bargain.

The commissar gets frustrated and angry in turn and threatens retribution. When this threat has no effect, he bursts out of the door with his two lieutenants and barks orders. His men straighten, discard their cigarettes, station themselves around their vehicle and raise their rifles waist-high pointing outwards. The commissar is helped up into the back of his truck. He stands looking confidently around the square with his hands on hips and his unsheathed sabre hanging loosely from his left hand and right hand on his still-holstered pistol. The committee orders the church bell to be rung, as had previously been arranged, for such an emergency.

The commissar and his men start and stare up at the tower across the square, as a single loud clang strikes and then fades. Rifles are held more purposefully, although there is yet no one except women and children for them to aim at. The uninvited visitors relax a little.

The chiming becomes regular. On another day, it would have been a call to worship. Bells ring in answer from neighbouring villages. Mothers hustle their children inside. Sophia does the same to Tamara and Isa.

'Go down into the cellar and hide. Stay till I call you.'

The girls go to do as they are told but get curious and instead sneak back into the front room and peep through the shutters. The mothers come out again and stand with folded arms watching in little groups. A few older village men come out from their houses with their farm tools. Two, positioned by the girl's window, have shotguns that they hold inconspicuously at their sides. As the bell rings louder and more urgently men come running from nearby fields. Others charge in on horse-back and by horse and cart, arriving from further away, with the produce they have been harvesting tumbling out. Their numbers grow, and the villagers get bolder. They shake their makeshift weapons in the air and start to shout in untidy unison for the evil-looking visitors to get out.

'Raus, raus, raus!' (German - Out, out, out!)

The Red militia, who had driven into the square in a show of strength, now stand in a circle round their truck and appear uncertain. They swing their bayoneted rifles from side-to-side at the surrounding villagers. The commissar stands in the back of the troop-carrier, brandishing his sabre and pointing his pistol in the farmers' faces. He shouts for the villagers to hold back, or he will order his men to shoot. This threat only increases the anger of the growing crowd. The shouts and curses intensify and the mob presses even closer, the long pitchforks almost touching the noses of the intruders.

There is a shot. One of the black-leather men has lost control. Then chaos. A quick, loud rattle of shots[6]. A roar. The farmers press in on all sides, hacking with spades, axes, and butcher's cleavers, stabbing with hayforks. Shouts, oaths and cries. Two White officers charge in slicing with their sabres. The dogs add to the noise and commotion, barking and running in circles around the melee.

It becomes quiet. The crowd backs off, some villagers shocked at what they have done, but more are triumphant and pump the air with weapons held high. The dogs now bark only sporadically, one bark at a time. The dead militiamen lie around their truck, cut-up and bloodied, a pitchfork stuck deep into the chest of one facing the girls. The commissar is hanging out of his vehicle backwards. One of the requisitioning squad is lying in the dust moving slowly and moaning. A village girl kneels down and places his head on her lap. A White officer nudges her aside, takes his pistol, and shoots him through the temple. Three dead villagers are carried to the community hall. Other villagers are standing, talking excitedly but quietly. Most have blood on them and on their farmyard weapons. Some are limping or holding wounds. The women rush to their men, although not all the wives are there, as a few men have come from surrounding villages. These look lost at first but are quickly noticed, and someone comes to give care and comfort. Curious and excited dogs are shooed away. A cockerel crows and is answered from the distance by another.

Tamara and Isa creep out of hiding and see dead bodies lying in the square. They have never seen anyone dead before, and Tamara wonders why they keep their mouths open and stare. The girls are

---

[6] Later examination of the militia's rifles showed they were single-shot Berdan II weapons, which explains why there was not more, shooting.

noticed and hastily pushed inside. Through the shutters, they see how the black-clad bodies are loaded like sacks on to their truck. They sneak out yet again and hide between two houses to watch. This time everyone is too busy to notice. The villagers are tidying up and picking up the pieces left behind; hats, other bits of clothing, weapons and also pieces of flesh. Tamara suggests to Isa that they should help, and together they lift a big black bloodied boot up to the truck. Tamara has to walk backwards to drag a heavy sabre to the truck with its point scratching a wavy line in the blood and dust. She hears a squeak behind her and turns to see little sister looking, with her hands to her mouth, at a severed ear. But she coolly picks it up and holds it, palms up, just as she had done with the horrible toad they had found on the estate fruit orchard two years ago when she was only seven She walks like this to the truck and reaches up to present it to the farmer. He takes it with a finger and thumb, says,

'Bless you, sweetheart.' But drops it carelessly into a corner of the truck.

Seven men carrying spades and pickaxes follow the truck as it drives slowly out of the square. Tamara asks a neighbour where they are going, and she explains that all evidence of the fight must be buried and hidden as quickly as possible. The women do their best to clean the yard with buckets of water, rakes and stiff brooms. The village square, with its parallel rake markings in the dust, is now almost too clean and tidy to be real.

Sophia comes hurrying towards the girls. She has been busy bandaging the wounded villagers and is shocked to see the blood on them. She grabs Isa rather roughly by the hand and, with fingers and thumb pressed into the back of Tamara's neck, guides them to the village pump. Others are there, tending wounds and wringing out pieces of bloodied clothing into pools filled with red-stained water.

After the two are more or less clean, Sophia sits exhausted, elbows on knees, looking down, head in her hands, on the end of the wet wooden bench by the pump. But not for long.

She raises her head, pulls the girls close and looks them in the eyes.

'Are you alright?' Then, after both nod with Isa looking sideways at Tamara,

'Are you sure?' Again they nod together. Mama's eyes well, and she blinks. She clasps their heads, one after the other, with her hands over their ears, so it hurts and fiercely kisses each hard on both cheeks.

'You must be safe!'

She stands up, straightens her skirt, takes Isa in her right hand, gently this time, and crooks her left elbow tightly into Tamara's. They walk like this back to the cottage, Sophia hugging Tamara's arm close under her elbow. The two girls pick their way bare-footed in their knickers and vests with wet bundles pressed close to their chests and shoes dangling from fingers. All around the villagers are tidying up and trying to get back to normal. There are a few hurried greetings and enquiries as to whether anyone in the family has been hurt. Everyone is busy, and no one gives them strange looks.

Tamara leans across, in front of Sophia as they go and whispers to Isa, 'Mademoiselle would never have allowed us to walk dressed like this in Alexander Park.'

Chapter 11 – Towards Kleinliebental

Paul and Sophia realise it is not going to be safe to stay in Grossliebental, as the Reds will be back. There will be reprisals. They and a few other refugees decide to move to the nearest German colony village of Kleinliebental. There is yet another sorting out of essential items. When moving from their Marazlievskaya apartment to Mrs Van Dych's Paul had included both large, heavy and delicate valuable items that they hoped to be able to take back when things improved. Travelling to Grossliebental from Mrs Van Dych, Paul had limited himself to only those things the family needed to survive. Now he excludes yet further items but still includes clothing for all weathers. They have no idea how long they will be on the run. He takes as much food as he can gather and then the papers; identity papers, title deeds, property plans, bonds, cash and valuables that might have to be bartered. He does not allow a single stick of furniture, so when they stop for a rest, they sit on the ground.

No horses are available so a group of twelve, pushing one largish and a smaller hand-cart set off on foot. There are several other family members. Paul's oldest brother Uncle Albert and his wife Aunty Mathilda (Tilla) and another Uncle Albert - Albert Linke with his family.

It is a journey of about fifteen kilometres by road. However, they decide it will be safer to go cross-country to avoid the military. As they walk, they can hear the sounds of continuing skirmishes. If they see movement in the distance, they lie down and hide behind the hay-ricks or bushes. They have no way of knowing whether those far off are other refugees, friendly farmers of the Green militia, dangerous Bolsheviks or marauding anarchists. The children, dressed as peasants, are bare-footed and are soon crying as the stubble bites into the soles of their feet. They are given turns on the carts, but this only makes it more difficult for those already tired from pushing and pulling.

Although the Ukraine is thought of as being flat steppe, the route is intersected by several small gullies, some dry in this summer season, others, still with water, that run into the Suchoy Estuary on which Kleinliebental is situated. They come to yet another dry, rocky, gully and have the usual difficulty in controlling the cart, as it is in danger of tipping over and shedding its load on the way down. As the four men set about pushing it up the other side, the two Uncle Alberts have a healthy debate as to whether to leave it behind or not. It is not quite an argument, and it is a difficult decision. In the gullies, it is an encumbrance. However, on the flat grass fields, it is a great aid and allows them to progress at a normal walking pace. The thought of having to lug a varied mix of possessions on their shoulders leads to a decision to keep the cart. They need to negotiate only one more gully before they enter a flatter landscape.

Two pairs of swans eye the party warily as it approaches along the side of a drainage dyke. One pair lifts itself noisily and laboriously into the air. The other two slide slowly into the water and then turn to face the group and observe it as if to say, 'you can't get us now.'

Paul thinks, 'If only I had my gun with me.'

All in the little group step carefully to avoid the sticky dog-size droppings among the white feathers, where the swans have created a convenient gap in the reeds for launching themselves into the water. Isa asks Sophia why the swans poo on the land and make such a mess.

'They should do it in the water.'

'I don't know. Ask your father.'

She does, 'Papa ......'

'Would you want to drink the water in which you have just done your business? 'Is his reply.

The family receive a warm welcome when they arrive tired and frightened at Kleinliebental. It is a Catholic village, but there is a strong camaraderie between the local colonies that had participated in the execution of the thieving, over-demanding Bolshevik-requisitioning party. Tamara realises, and tells Isa, that this is one of the villages that Mama had pointed out to them from the top of the cemetery hill in Grossliebental.

The next morning they hear crying. The body of a neighbour's son has been brought in from Grossliebental. He had died later of his wounds. The villagers are now expecting - and preparing to defend themselves against - the punitive force that they expect to be sent against them. There is a local alliance between Grossliebenthal itself, Kleinliebental, Alexanderhilf, Lustdorf on the coast and other smaller villages, including, also Russian and Ukrainian. The revolt of the colonies, against Red oppression and demands for supplies and men for the Red Army, spreads widely to many other villages; ranging from Worms, 125 km north-east, to the Hoffnungstal group of villages, 99 km to the north-west.

News arrives that the expected, heavily-armed, Red Army force is advancing towards the Liebental villages. Paul tells Sophia it is his duty to volunteer to support the freedom fight. He says it is the last chance the colony villages have of beating the Bolshevik revolutionaries. She is horrified at his decision. They have survived together this far. Why must he risk it all now? But she keeps her thoughts and fears to herself. The two Alberts, both being well over ten years older than Paul, decide not to volunteer. At least not yet. They will stay and look after the wives and children. Paul is happy with their decision, and Sophia is comforted to have them with her.

Next day Paul says his good-byes. He embraces and kisses Sophia, tells her to be brave and promises to return soon. He tells the girls to be good, to look after Mama and to study hard. He then joins a group of about thirty villagers, plus three White Army officers, on the march back again to Grossliebental. They do not march as a military unit. They look like one of the many of refugee bands that now roam the countryside, vainly seeking sanctuary, but this band is all men and a few, if one looks closely, can be seen to be carrying weapons.

Chapter 12 – Battle of the Villagers

The Bolshevik forces arrive on the outskirts of Grossliebental on 5th August and find the villagers in higher numbers and much better prepared than they had predicted. Instead of carrying out a quick destruction of the village and the sample execution of a number of the men, they become involved in a bloody battle in which neither side gains a quick victory. One of the villager's early and vital successes is the breaking of the railway line to Odessa that provides supplies from Kiev to the Bolsheviks.

This effective joint village resistance encourages White Army support, and a proper front is established, under the command of General Schöll. The front stretches from the Black Sea to a hundred, and more, kilometres inland.

A call for further volunteers goes out. Paul is one of those who responds. As all collect together, both inside and outside the Grossliebental community hall, he finds himself in very diverse company. He is not the only bourgeois volunteer. There are a dentist and two senior Odessa civil officials, one of whom Paul knows, as they have had dealings together on the setting up of his Mercedes showroom.

'Pavel Fredrikovich, what is happening to us? When will this madness end? I didn't plan to become a soldier. But here we are, having to defend home and family.'

There are many small farmers, some of who own land, others who do not. These, last would have either worked for others or rented fields on which to grow crops. Some villagers in this group are now supporting the Reds in the hope of being given land, as promised in the Red propaganda. Other colonist farmers have formed militia groups, commonly known as the *Greens,* to defend their properties and have already joined in skirmishes against the Bolsheviks. These amateur soldiers are supported by a scattering of professionals from the Tsar's army, who have emerged from hiding in the villages.

The volunteers are asked if they can shoot and, if they answer, in the affermative are handed a rifle. As ammunition is in short supply, no practices are planned. Real targets will present themselves soon enough. Paul, like others, is issued with the standard Russian Mosin-Nagant M1891 rifle, used by the Tsarist forces from 1896. It is now, also the primary weapon of the Red army. He wishes for his Belgian Frankotte hunting rifle, stolen during the move out of Odessa, which is lighter and would be more accurate. However, that this Mosin-Nagant, has a magazine of five shots and the ability to fire more quickly, has to be an advantage in battle.

He is full of anger and keen to get his revenge on the Reds that have stolen his property and are hounding him and his family. As he is handed his weapon, he is nevertheless shocked by the realisation that he is now preparing to kill human beings and not just a stag or a wild boar. There is excitement and urgency. All know there is danger, but all also want to use this opportunity of fighting back against the Reds, instead of meekly acceding to their overburdening demands.

Without training or instruction, Paul is allocated to a squad tasked with taking out of action one and, if possible, two cannons. These are located somewhat ahead of the main enemy line and hindering the advance of the Whites in the area. There are just seven in the squad; first a young White Army lieutenant in charge supported by a veteran White Army corporal. The young lieutenant reminds Paul of the one he got to know at Mrs Van Dyke's and, like that officer, has also torn off his regimental and ranking insignia, in fear of discovery by the Reds. The rest of the squad are small farmers wishing to defend their stock and land from confiscation by the Reds. Although in the past they would have used their guns only to shoot vermin and game, these had already fought as Greens in guerrilla raids against the Reds. Paul is the least experienced of the group, in warfare.

The officer views the two cannon positions through his field glasses. It appears that both are minimally manned, having just the number required to load and fire their artillery. Either the Reds are short of men, or they do not consider that a direct raid on their positions is likely. That is good news. The officer plans to go right up to the enemy line and to approach the first cannon position from the side. He crawls with his small patrol to a low bluff, from where he intends to attack, and surveys it with his field glasses once more. He confirms it is manned by the minimum complement of just five gunners. There is no look-out or guard. All are engrossed in the process of loading aiming and firing. The cannon is an M1877 direct-fire field-gun, mounted on large cart-like wheels and would have been drawn by horses. The barrel is fixed to its mounting, and each time it is fired, it rolls back. The Gunners have to reposition it again after each round. So the firing rate is slow.

In spite of his inexperience, Paul is placed in charge of two farmers and assigned the role of providing covering fire, from the bluff where they are crouching. The remaining four form the storming party. Led by the White officer, they crawl through the covering ferns and brush, down the bluff on all fours or on their bellies, to get as close as possible to the cannon position without being seen.

When they are less than a hundred metres from their target, the officer cautiously raises an arm as the signal for Paul and his comrades to open heavy fire. This they do. Paul aims, and it registers that this is his first human target. His first shot misses but he can see it went to the right. His sights are slightly out. He corrects his aim, and his next shot is true. He experiences the same feeling of triumph as when achieving the perfect hit on a stag. This, though, is mixed with shame and remorse at killing a fellow human. His guilt lessens as the skirmish progresses. His hunting experience is relevant, and his aim true. He waits patiently for even a part of a defender to show and then firmly squeezes the trigger. When the Red defenders are fully engaged, either in hiding from - or in returning - the fire, the officer leads the raiding party charge, sabre aloft, the others with bayonets fixed, shooting and shouting as they run. Paul is now so confident of his aim that he continues firing into the melee, knowing he can hit the enemy without wounding one of his own.

As soon as the forward party are fully engaged, Paul and his two companions follow, charging, yelling, down the slope with weapons at the ready. The other two have attached bayonets. Although it is compulsory to have these fitted during battle, Paul does not.

As they get close a Red gunner runs, trying to escape. Paul, still on the move, shoots from the hip. Something he has never done before but nevertheless hits him square in the back. The wounded man falls and then struggles to get up, but the officer takes a few quick steps and shoots him in the head. Paul gasps but says nothing. This is a cruel, nasty war. Paul looks more closely at the executed soldier He is wearing a tattered German army uniform, plus red material flashes roughly sewn on. He rummages quickly in the dead man's top pockets and finds the photograph of a pretty, fair-haired girl, plus identification papers proving he is, indeed, German. So now he has shot a fellow countryman. As the battle progresses, Paul is both angered and saddened to discover that there are many ethnic Germans among the opposing Bolshevik force. These are Spartakists. They include the formerly unemployed and disfranchised from the colony villages. But most appear to be ex-prisoners of the war against the Tsar, who have been released by the Bolsheviks, and who choose to desert the German army and join the Reds, rather than return to their homeland.

All five enemy are now dead with the raiding unit suffering only two small skin wounds between them. It would seem, from the ease with which they have won their first objective that the Red guards are even less prepared for battle than their attackers.

After quickly applying rough bandages, the officer orders his team to turn the captured cannon to the right, towards the neighbouring cannon position in the enemy line. He is working with men who have never been close to a field-gun before, let alone aimed, loaded and fired one. Paul admires that the young officer does not lose patience and recognises he is working with inexperienced but motivated beginners and, although urging speed, he does not shout but explains as clearly as he can precisely what is needed. His corporal is a huge help. The lieutenant's first language is Russian whereas the farmers usually speak German, so Paul interprets when necessary. Slowly, the cannon is turned, and the barrel lowered to almost horizontal without the enemy realising the threat that is developing. It requires only two rounds, with a gap in-between longer than the officer would have liked, to persuade the Reds to abandon their position and to run in panic from the short-range cannon attack. This inexperienced team has overrun two cannon positions. They are exultant. A messenger is sent off with an urgent request for additional support to man the newly captured weapons.

As the battle develops, Paul establishes himself as a sniper. He manages to acquire a German Mauser Gewehr 98 with a times three magnification telescopic sight. Paul can't avoid a sad smile as he takes ownership. Before, a German sniper it will have used it against the Russian Tsarist forces, now it is to be fired in Russia's internal war. Paul hides himself in strategic locations, much as he would have done on a hunt. Then it might have been a small wooden hide constructed in a tree. In this war, it is typically the attic window of a war-damaged village house. A high window in a church steeple is ideal but suffers from the danger that it is readily identified. In any case, he cannot stay long in any one position, as snipers are naturally hated and feared, and as soon as their location becomes known, heavy artillery is directed at them. Paul picks off the enemy when they are careless and show themselves. This role suits him. He somehow feels that, even under direct threat from the hated Bolsheviks, he would not be able to stab a fellow human through the chest with a bayonet. Paul often stays at his post overnight sitting or crouching in his nest, wrapped in a blanket, waiting for a careless Red to silhouette himself against the sky or to light a cigarette.

A young boy of only thirteen, or so, is given the role of supplying Paul with ammunition, food and importantly water. They become close, and Paul shares his food rations. One day there is no boy. First, he worries about his low ammunition store. He has no food left but sufficient water for a day or two. Then he worries about the boy. Next day an even younger boy arrives, probably nine or ten. From his looks, Paul guesses he is the brother.

'Where is your brother?'

'He's dead, Sir. Shot, Sir.'

Tears are in his eyes, but he refuses to cry and stands erect, forgetting to put down his heavy load.

'Put that load down and get down yourself! Don't expose yourself! You should not be here. You're too young.'

'My mother says I must, and I want to. She says father is out fighting and we must win this war or we'll lose all our animals, our farm and our land, everything. Then we might as well all be dead.'

Paul shares his lunch with his new companion. He pleads internally that none of his targets has been as young.

The front advances slowly, and Paul's new young powder monkey is as efficient and punctual as his brother had been.

The supply of ammunition becomes erratic and less generous. Could he soon be squatting at his post with no rounds left to fire? The shortage is a forewarning of a general problem along the front for, on the 12th August, only four weeks following the uprising in Odessa, comes the devastating command from General Schöll's HQ, to abandon the battle. They are ordered to scatter and to destroy any weapons that cannot be kept from the enemy. No official reason is given, but it is soon confirmed that a shortage of munitions is the cause. Rumour is that, although the Romanians just across the border have a plentiful supply, they are frightened to sell any to the Whites; the Bolsheviks having threatened that they will advance across the Dniester if they do so.

Rather than spiking[7] the valuable cannons, as ordered, Paul's team optimistically buries them in the hope that the war will reverse yet again and that they can then recover and re-deploy them. They use two large mortar craters to reduce the work of excavation needed.

---

[7] Term used for putting armament out of use. Comes from the medieval practice of hammering a spike into the touch-hole of a canon to render it useless.

Chapter 13 – West to Franzfeld

It is an anti-climax and a colossal disappointment for Paul to have to give up so suddenly after their initial successes and simply to return to his family and to his role as a fleeing refugee. Although the fighting is brutal and harsh, he much prefers to be doing that in the cause of freedom than to be running from the Bolsheviks like a frightened coward. Sophia though is happy and relieved to have him back. Sporadic fighting continues, and canon and gunfire can be heard clearly in Kleinliebental, sometimes getting closer and then again fading. The girls are now crying with fear.

Paul suggests to Sophia that they should flee still further west and aim for the Catholic village of Franzfeld on the River Dniester that forms the boundary with land now under Romanian control. The plan would be to escape across the river and then to travel by whatever means possible to Germany. Paul retrieves his knapsack with their important papers and valuables, and they form a smaller party than before, made up of just family members plus Monsieur Eterin, the Swiss Vice-consul in Odessa. It is a sign of the hardening of the Bolshevik attitude that a Swiss foreigner is no longer sure that his neutrality will keep him safe. They plan to take just one small hand wagon.

At the last moment, Paul decides that they must delay a day. He gets the village carpenter to create a false bottom in the cart. It must be made of old wood, so it is not apparent that an alteration has been made, and still allow light to be seen between the planks when looked at from above. The carpenter rises to the challenge of getting one over the Bolsheviks and does an excellent job. There is space enough for the few essential documents, coins, paper money and jewellery. Paul and Sophia worry how Tamara and Isa will survive the hardships of the much longer forty-kilometre trek. As a result of their last experience, there is no argument when the girls plead to be allowed to keep their shoes on. In any case, theirs are now as scuffed as those of any of the village children.

Their journey starts west, back towards and past Grossliebental. It is more challenging than their earlier eastward journey as, with the Reds in occupation, they need to give the town a wide berth. Sophia thinks what a shame it was to have travelled to Kleinliebental, only to have to go all that way back past Grossliebental again. It is hard for the adults and even worse for the children. The fleeing refugees can tell that skirmishes are still going on as they can hear guns and the louder canon fire. A stray shell falls too close and explodes. When it seems the battle is getting closer, they march faster or detour from their chosen route. They come across the same frustrating gullies as before but know better how to negotiate them, and their load is much less. They are now more experienced trekkers and take only the essential items. Again they keep away from the roads along which military traffic might be passing and hide if they see movement in the distance.

Halfway through the day, as the party is walking along a water dyke, there is movement on the bank above them. A man on horseback is silhouetted against the sky. He has a rifle over his shoulder and crossed bandoliers over his chest. A second man on foot appears, also heavily armed and then another, and another. The little party of refugees are uncertain what to do and carry on slowly along the dyke. The militia group on the bank above has grown to about a dozen.

The horseman raises a hand and shouts, 'Halt! Stoyi!' ('Stop,' said first in German, then in Russian)

The refugees come to an uncoordinated stop. What else can they do? The band above them is heavily armed. But it is as ragged as the refugees themselves.

The leader gets down from his horse and hands the reins to another. He waves his hand over his shoulder for someone to join him and the two walk through the long, browning grass, down to the Vaatz family group.

'Who are you?' He asks in German. Where are you going? Why?

Paul and both Alberts move forward.

Paul asks in return, 'And who are you?'

'We're farmers fighting to protect our farms and families.'

'And we are families running from Grossliebental where the Reds are destroying our village.'

'What food have you got?'

'Practically none. Not enough for ourselves. We hope, when we get to Franzfeld, they will be able to feed us.'

This interaction takes place with the women close by, listening silently, and with the wide-eyed girls, Isa with fingers to her mouth, wondering whether they should be frightened of these heavily armed strangers.

'My men are starving.' And then, 'What about that dog?' Pointing at Maxi.

No.' screams Tamara, with Isa joining in at the tail end of her shout. Tamara picks up Maxi, hugs him close and turns her back. Maxi tries to licks her face. Isa supports Tamara and consoles the dog.

'Have you no feelings' Don't you have children?

'I do, but these are hard times.' He does not apologise.

'We are also short of food. I am sorry, but we can't help, much as we support what you are doing.' Says Paul.

'We are armed. We can take what we want.'

'You can, but you won't get much, and you will be robbing those you wish to protect. I fought in that Grossliebental battle, and that's why we must run away. We had to give up that fight because we had no ammunition. I wish you success, but I don't see how you can win now.'

Brother Albert chips in, 'Let's, give them half our flour and some corncobs. It means we will go short and it will still not be enough for them, but it would be stupid for us to quarrel. We are on the same side, and we just have to hope that Franzfeld can feed us.'

He looks around the group. All nod slowly without enthusiasm, but it is agreed. The refugees hunt through their cart, and the contents of two sacks are adjusted and handed over to the Greens.

Civilised good-byes are said, polite handshakes given, and the two parties separate and go their ways, the Vaatz group relieved that their encounter with strangers has not been a seriously threatening one.

As they continue along the water-course, Sophia asks Paul to pick a few bulrushes for her. She has an idea for the girls. She also encourages them to collect wildflower samples for pressing. They can identify those she can't name when they get back to civilisation again. The flowers of the white convolvulus that climb profusely up the bulrushes are apparent candidates but, they discover, fade almost as soon as they are picked and are quickly discarded as candidates for pressing.

The first target destination is the colony village of Neuburg. This is about a quarter of the way along their journey and cannot be avoided, as it is where they must cross the River Baraboy. They start to worry whether there will be Red militia who might take an interest in them. There is a little conference, and to be less conspicuous, they agree to split into two groups. They will meet up again at the Franzfeld-Mayaki crossroads, which brother-in-law Albert says is about one kilometre the other side of the town.

Paul's family plus brother Albert and Mathilde go first with the cart and take the heavier belongings. The precious items have been carefully stowed in the new secret compartment. Albert Linke's family plus the Swiss consul will follow an hour later.

They enter Neuburg and are given an enquiring look by the first villagers they meet. A greeting in German is answered with a friendly reply and a question as to where they are going. Their story is that they hope to visit cousins in Franzfeld. Without asking, they are told that there is a guard of two soldiers on the bridge, also that they are the only soldiers in the village and are not particularly vigilant. Further, there is no guard after sunset. It is already getting dark, but they decide not to wait. The guards seem bored. The village is situated on both sides of the river, and villagers cross backwards and forwards all the time and are just waved through. Paul's demob document now has a red-star stamp on it together with a commissar's signature. This satisfies the guards. Brother Albert shows the identity document that served him well before. There is a quick rummage through the belongings in the cart. Paul gets the impression that they are searching for items that might be purloined rather than for incriminating evidence. Some wine or better, Vodka would no doubt have been welcome. They are waved on and remain on the road until they get to the crossroads. The way to Mayaki is sign-posted as going right. Just off the road, to the left, is a little copse, and they camp at its edge. The girls help to search for wood, and they light a small campfire. They brew tea and drink this with bread, but it is good rye, and they add some smoked sausage.

The rest arrive after dark, two hours later. They had received the same information, regarding the guard-post and decided it was worth waiting until the guards left their post, before crossing.

The children help to put down and straighten the waterproof oil sheets. All wrap their coats close around themselves. Blankets had been rejected, as not worth carrying, on the first leg of their journey to Grossliebental. While the air is still warm, they nevertheless feel the chill of the falling dew. Mary, the Linke's daughter, three years older than Tamara, comes to lie with her and Isa. They look up at the stars together, and she points out the constellations that she knows. Apart from Orion with his belt, they agree it is not easy to understand how the constellations get their names. The Great Bear should definitely be called the saucepan. Mary tells them to listen to the loud chirping of Cicadas, and they wonder how these manage, every now and again, to all go silent at the same time and to then start up again, together. They sleep surprisingly well.

In the morning, before seven, they are woken by trucks on the road. A Red army convoy is moving from Franzfeld towards Neuburg. Paul curses himself for being careless; they should have hidden themselves. Even the other side of the copse would have been enough. All get more nervous when the convoy stops and two men clamber out of the leading car and walk the fifty metres over the field towards them. Paul leaves their little campsite to meet them. One asks in Russian who they are and what are they doing here, and looks to his companion. The other starts to translate from Russian to German. Paul stands there as a humble peasant, head bowed and flat cap in hand, and lets him finish. Sophia has both hands in front of her mouth. She doesn't know whether to be frightened or to laugh. Paul is overacting, again. The one speaking first, by his authority and his uniform, is a Russian Bolshevik officer, probably from the north. The other is his interpreter. Paul explains, in a peasant German, that because of the fighting, they are taking their families to safety in Franzfeld. This is translated back.

The officer then says to his translator, in Russian, 'These refugees have children with them and are harmless. Tell them they should hurry as the fighting is likely to get worse and could well spread to here.'

Paul understands perfectly but remembers his role and lets the translator finish. Through the interpreter, he thanks the officer profusely and says they will set off straight away. The convoy drives off, no doubt to support the Reds in their battles around Grossliebental. Paul shocks Sophia by saying that given half a chance he would have shot that interpreter. He must have been a Spartakist traitor.

Although this turns out to be a harmless encounter, they decide it is still safer to continue their journey off-road. The families have to negotiate only one more gully before the land becomes quite flat and their speed of travel increases. This level terrain has its own obstacles. Where there is water, the reeds and bulrushes are head high. They start along a path on top of a dyke, all in single file, and each can only see the one or two in front. Then the trail peters out, it having been created by a fisherman solely to get to his favourite spot, where the reeds have been parted to give access to the water. They have to decide whether to press on in the hope they will re-connect with a path again, or to retrace their steps. There is not always agreement.

In the open fields, they see farm gates with no fences between which makes no sense. They quickly learn why when they try to take a short cut between two such gates and are confronted by a ditch. The ditches form practical animal barriers in this part of the country, and the gates are located where there are small bridges and crossing places.

Thorns are another challenge. Acacias seem to thrive here, from large spreading trees offering shade, to low bushes. But large or small all seem to have thorns. Some of the low shrubs, through which they consider pushing, have, nasty thorns, a full four centimetres long. When the travellers encounter these, they must make a detour. It would be serious if someone became infected.

As they walk, the sounds of battle become fainter and fainter. Now they hear nothing and feel they have made the right decision. They have another uneventful night in the open and arrive on their third evening in Franzfeld. It lies directly on the wide Dniester River estuary and is mainly a fishing - rather than a farming –village. It is much smaller than Grossliebental, with fewer than seven hundred inhabitants.

The travellers are relieved and happy to be so warmly received, even though their hosts are risking their lives and again are Catholics rather than Evangelicals. Tamara makes a face at the hot potato soup without salt that they are welcomed with but knows not to complain.

Paul's family is housed with the village cobbler. To minimise the chance of being recognised as a refugee from Grossliebenthal, which will now have a bad name with the Red forces because of the massacre, Paul assumes the role of an hostler. When a Red unit enters the village, he has to grab a broom and start mucking out the stables. Brother Albert, who is staying with a farmer, also becomes a flat-cap headed hostler. Brother-in-law is now just a simple farmer and helps in the fields as much as he can.

Already the next day, Paul makes enquires as to where and how they might find a boat to take them over the river. He quickly discovers that even with the offer of large sums of money, no one will help. The village head explains that this is not because of a lack of willingness or fear but because the Bolsheviks have destroyed all the boats they can find to stop refugees escaping across the River Dniester. If they do see anyone on the river, they shoot without warning.

This emphasises to Paul that, while they have escaped the dangers of the Bolshevik reprisals expected in the two Liebental villages, their journey west has taken them deep into Red territory. It is a depressing realisation. Most of the time, though, the atmosphere of fear is not as intense as in Odessa or in the two Liebental villages. The CheKa is far away.

Paul's family members each adjust differently to a village life that they had formerly experienced only as employers and patrons. Paul longs for his books and thinks wryly of them stacked away in Mrs Van Dych's storeroom. What use are they there? He makes an attempt to teach the girls, but typically his sessions end in tears. Although he loves them desperately, he is impatient and on edge and finds himself shouting at them.

He becomes morose and moody, worrying and planning for a way out of their nightmare but getting nowhere. He decides that rather than sitting around worrying, he should help the village men in their work. He realises it is perverse to rough up his hands and dirty his fingernails artificially, to satisfy the demands of a random inspection when he can harden them doing something useful. Soon he is chopping wood, feeding the pigs and hoeing the house vegetable patch. He finds it satisfying and therapeutic. The village men approve too and enjoy showing him how to do some of the chores more efficiently. On getting closer to the village men, Paul learns how the fishermen, who were in the majority, have also had to adjust because their boats have been destroyed. As they can no longer fish, they have to rely on their farming friends for work and help with caring for both animals and crops.

Sophia is better than Paul at being positive and cheerful and not overemphasising the danger they are in. She is quite successful in making an adventure of their hardships and manages to continue with the girls' lessons and also teaches some of the village children reading and writing. In this, she has to be careful not to make herself too noticeable as the Red soldiers who wander freely around the village could become suspicious of any unusual activity.

The girls understand the Bolsheviks are evil and that they had to run away. However, provided they get fed, they adapt surprisingly well. Their bare feet are now hardened, and they play cheerfully with the village children. Tamara, being older, senses the danger more. She finds it difficult to forget that she is of land-owning stock and tends to use her authority to organise the children's games. At almost thirteen and one of the oldest children in the village, she usually gets away with this. Tamara also plays teacher and makes some progress in teaching village children the alphabet and how to write their names in the dust. Sophia has to warn her, though, that teaching French is not a good idea. Isa is more relaxed and carefree, and when there is no immediate danger plays happily with the village children as equals.

Chapter 14 – Jewellery Bag and a Snake

Things become quieter, but the Reds are always around and, although the militia is not as extreme and vicious as the CheKa, they are unpredictable and dangerous enough.

Mathilda has managed to obtain a small bag of flour and is walking alone back to their lodgings dressed, as always, as a farmer's wife, when she is stopped and questioned by a suspicious and somewhat drunken Bolshevik sailor. He discovers her bag of flour and loudly accuses her of *speculating*. Speculation[8] being a crime in Bolshevik eyes, punishable by death. She explains it is not for sale but for her husband. As soon as she mentions her husband, she realises she has put Albert's life at risk as well as her own, for around her neck is a small bag of jewellery. This includes the ruby and diamond Fabergé cufflinks that Albert had received for his 21st birthday. Although she had bartered her earrings, she had managed to avoid exchanging the cufflinks for food during their trek through the German colonies. If her accuser finds the bag, both will be shot.

The sailor orders her to follow him to the Red guard-post for interrogation. As he is leading and not watching her, she somehow manages to get the little bag from around her neck and throw it into the hedge. The sailor notices a movement and angrily demands to

---

[8] 'Speculation' is one of the many ill-defined 'crimes' used by the Bolsheviks to accuse their adversaries. It can be interpreted to include any form of private trading.

know what she is doing. She apologises and explains that she tripped. He is not convinced, inspects her hands, pats her down and examines the sleeves of her coat. He gives a suspicious grunt and then places her in front, pushing her roughly on the shoulders, now and again, towards the guard post. Albert is hauled in, and both are aggressively questioned and searched.

Tilla jumps when they find Albert's identity pass. Any entry indicating he is a landowner or that he had any status at all will be his death warrant and possibly hers.

Mathilda sees Albert's relaxed face and remembers he had told her how, at the last renewal, his occupation had been entered as *farm-worker* and not *farm-owner*. This was at the advice of a friendly Tsarist police officer when things had started to become difficult. Albert had at first tried to reject this advice, proud to keep his status, but luckily had been persuaded, as this false-genuine pass, with all its proper stamps and signatures, saved both their lives. With many a *tovarich* (comrade) this and *tovarich* that, they leave the guard post, locked arm-in-arm and still with the precious little bag of flour.

Having got over the shock, Mathilda is desperate to get her jewellery back but is too frightened to return to the same place. However, two days later, when the Red pressure seems to be less, the host's fifteen-year-old son volunteers to search for her precious bag. He returns triumphant having found it stuck in the low branches of a bush exactly where she had said. He is somewhat embarrassed to be so warmly hugged and kissed by Paul's grateful sister-in-law.

***

As Paul is resting in the cobbler's house, trying to relax after their life-threatening experiences and dreaming of possible means of escape, the owner rushes in urging him to leave, 'Now!'

Paul is too much of a risk. A Red militia unit is entering the village, and some men are due to be billeted in his house. He does not know for how long. Paul's wife and children can stay. If the Reds find Paul, the cobbler is frightened, that both he and Paul will be shot. Paul quickly grabs his flat hat and a hoe, and as he goes out the back door, the visitors drive noisily into the yard at the front. Paul starts to hoe the plot close to the house. To add to his disguise, he has taken off his glasses and rolls and smokes a cheap Peoples' cigarette. Gradually he hoes closer to the edge of the garden and nearer to the rushes by the river and when he thinks no one was looking, jumps into the reeds and hides. After a while, Paul raises his head and peeps out. Other heads pop up and hide quickly again. So he is not alone. All are very nervous because close-by Red soldiers are watering their horses in the river and singing their threatening revolutionary songs. He squats uncomfortably on the damp ground for several hours.

It is just getting dark when he sees a fat grey snake come sliding silently through the reeds. It appears to be aiming for his feet. He has severe ophiophobia and cannot stop himself from giving a loud yelp and jumping up out of the reed-bed without thinking of Bolsheviks or anything else. Shocked, both by his experience with the snake and the stupidity of leaping out without checking, he crouches down, is still and listens. Luckily for him, there is no one near, and the horse-watering duties have finished.

He assumes it will not be safe to return to the house and decides to wander cautiously along the river-bank to the edge of Franzfeld where they had passed on the way in, as he knows his friend, Aksel is hiding there. He finds him sitting dejectedly on a straw bale. Both are pleased to see each other and prepare to overnight together. Paul thinks this is safer as he does not know when the Reds will be leaving the cobbler's house. He cannot let Sophia know as Reds are billeted everywhere - in nearly every home. As the pair try to sleep the mice and the rats run over and around them, but Paul does not care so long as there are no snakes.

The next morning Paul checks that the visiting Reds have gone and goes urgently to Sophia. But he finds her seriously ill. She had worried because he had not returned as soon as the Reds left and spent all night walking backwards and forwards along the river bank shouting his name. She was convinced he had been discovered and shot. She had caught a severe chill and suffered Angina from which she might have died.

Paul begs a cart and, even though it is August and warm, has to wrap her in a blanket. He takes her the ten kilometres up Dniester estuary to the small Ukrainian town of Mayaki to find a doctor. This is risky as it is full of Revolutionaries, and Paul worries that the doctor might be a Red or a Jew. He discovers the surgery just off the village square. Which is not good as that is where the off-duty militia tends to gather. The doctor senses his nervousness, and they hide the horse and cart behind the house.

Sophia is put to bed, and they stay for four full days. Paul is allowed to sleep in an armchair by her bed. The doctor's wife feeds them mostly on soup and potatoes. One day she manages a boiled corncob to share. At first, the doctor will take nothing for the care, but Paul insists. As they leave Paul notices, through an open door, the small Hanukkah menorah on the mantelpiece. So the doctor is Jewish. Paul concedes to Sophia that he would have been nervous, had he known before. The fact is that he took great care of Sophia, and she quickly recovered. Paul admits to himself that there are good Jews. As he does so, he realises how irrational this awful Revolution has made everyone. In Odessa almost half the doctors are Jewish. Why was he worrying? His regular doctor was a Jew. He had looked after the whole family very well and had supervised Isa's birth.

In this way, the three refugee families have to spend their time dressed as poor farmers and always at risk of being discovered and shot. Paul has hidden his incriminating and precious items under straw bales in the farmer's house, and they will stay there until they can leave Franzfeld. The Bolshevik swine must not discover them, he thinks. He has no real concern about being exposed by the Franzfeld villagers even though his family are strangers and villagers are at considerable risk. All the Germans hold together, and as for the rest he trusts on the will and bounty of the Almighty. Paul's family sleep on the straw-covered lime floor. Beetles and other insects crawl everywhere, but luckily there are no fleas or lice to torment them.

There is an unexpected diversion when the headman reveals that two boats will be permitted to go out and fish. He has persuaded the local Red non-commissioned officer in charge, to allow them to repair two of the many boats destroyed to stop refugees escaping across the river. The agreement is that the fishermen stay within a hundred metres of the shore and that the catch will be halved between the villagers and the Red Army unit. This is not a fair division as the regular army unit in the village is less than a dozen. The girls are not the only ones to watch this surprise event. Most of those villagers who do not have to go out into the fields are there. Three militia stand on the river bank with loaded guns to ensure the agreement is not broken. Occasionally there is a warning shout for a boat to stay closer, but the general mood is unusually friendly. There is a pretty good catch, perhaps because the river has not been fished for so long. The militia is generous and allows the villagers to take more than the agreed half of the catch. That evening the family enjoy an unusually tasty and nourishing supper with the villagers. There are even fish over that are carefully preserved for an uncertain future.

Paul ponders how the atmosphere in this village is so different from that in the Liebental colonies. Here the villagers have reached an accommodation with their conquerors. The main benefit is that their village is still intact. There are no destroyed houses. They pay the price, as they have to give the Reds all they want. However, they can keep the rest of their produce and so far they have not had to starve. He doubts whether anyone has been shot. Although they do have to make room for the resident militia and sometimes must host and feed larger units passing through, by and large, the villagers live in their own houses. Luckily, it seems, that by the time that he and his family arrived the Reds had already finished off all the wine and vodka that had been stored in the cellars. A drunken Bolshevik can be very dangerous, as Paul had seen in Odessa. He was told that the villagers did not make much Vodka, as that is not a favoured drink. At times, when he is very depressed, he wonders whether this policy of non-resistance is not a wiser strategy.

Chapter 15 – The Firewood Pile

The frightening news arrives that a CheKa search party is scouring the surrounding area searching for the Vaatz family, which they have been informed is in the area. To know that the CheKa is now hunting specifically for the Vaatz family, not just any Bourgeois is an awful shock to Paul and Sophia. It worries the villagers too, as they realise that their own risk is heightened. The village has survived, so far, by following a policy of appeasement. Many do not want to change this. They realise that they are harbouring a living, walking death threat.

There are murmurs, 'Why should we get ourselves shot for hiding rich strangers who we hardly know?'

But the head of the village, Hilsendeger, is firm. 'We have a duty to save our countrymen.'

He creates a hiding place, a storeroom in his own house in Grossgaessel, on the village square. The headman and two friends arrange a large, heavy cupboard so it can quickly be pushed into place to hide the door. He asks other villagers to help increase the height of the firewood pile stacked against the outside wall to conceal the small window of the room. They bring food, water and rugs to put inside. There is also a bucket. All this is done very quickly. Look-outs are sent away to warn of the approach of the CheKa search party. Maxi is given into the care of one of the villagers, who has children who play with Tamara and Isa. It would be perverse if he was to lead the CheKa to the hiding place.

Paul is surprised and overwhelmed with gratitude at Hilsendeger's firmness and that he has been able to persuade the surprisingly few reluctant villagers, also to agree.

Already, in the middle of the following day, two boys, of not more than ten or eleven years old, rush into the square, out of breath and seeking out the village head.

'Die Roten kommen,' ('The Reds are coming.') is their message.

The search party is already well on its way from Mayaki on the River Dniester to the north. Had the unit continued in their truck, the CheKa party would have beaten the boy messengers to the village, which would have been a disaster. Fortunately, when the boys saw them they had halted under a tree to eat.

The refugees are hustled into the cramped hiding place. It becomes totally dark as the door is shut. There are grunts as men drag the large cupboard into place. Outside there is chattering and activity, and Paul works out that dust is being scattered over the floor to disguise the scrape marks that the cupboard has left. Paul's family, his brother and wife and the Linke family need to sort themselves. Tamara and Isa are not at all happy. The young boy cousins make a good show of being brave. Each family settles in a corner. The grown-ups sit with their backs to the wall their feet touching in the centre. The smaller children sit on laps. Brother Albert lights a candle to help them see and organise. Sophia starts to tell a story to cheer the children, but they are hardly listening. They realise they are *living* a story - a nightmare.

Paul sits, in the dark, on the rough wooden floorboards beside Sophia, who has Isa on her knees. On the other side, his arm is around Tamara. The burden of responsibility for their care and future weighs heavily. He is not comfortable having to wait for events to happen. He must do something. But what? He should be out fighting. But on whose side? The Germans have already lost, and the Tsar has been assassinated. There is hushed intermittent whispering, mostly to comfort the children. But there is also silence in the darkness with both adults and children sitting quietly with their thoughts. Paul's mind wanders to the past.

Paul dreams – Mercedes

Things had been so exciting and positive so very recently. Everything had started well. In Sophia, he had found the perfect wife. She loved, encouraged and supported him. He had two sweet and wonderful girls. They could be naughty and lazy at times, but they were bright and cheerful and must not come to harm.

He had embarked on a risky business adventure, with no experience and against the advice and arguments of friends and family. The German colonists' mantra was to invest in land - and more land. Land, they reasoned did not age, could neither be destroyed nor stolen. It would not burn. It lasted forever. Sadly, they were wrong, but he was faring no better with his business. Now the family had nothing. They would be lucky to live, and at this moment it appeared entirely possible that they would not.

While still a student at the University of Antwerp, he had visited the Exposition de l'Industrie that was taking place. Among many other exciting exhibits, DMG (*Daimler Motoren Gesellschaft*) was displaying their prototype Mercedes motorcar. It was very different from the horseless carriage images shown in the journals and newspapers he had read recently. The engine was not just stuck on to a traditional horse carriage structure. It had been integrated into the vehicle. Paul had been impressed with the demonstration he had been given and was exhilarated by the feel of the wind in his face. The salesman was enthusiastic but somewhat condescending of the potential of this eager, young student client. Paul had enquired about availability in Russia and was told that this would be complicated and expensive. He had persisted and asked for the cost and delivery of a similar car. The salesman was dubious as to whether this was a genuine lead but promised to obtain a quote. This arrived directly from Stuttgart, some three weeks later and Paul had placed his order. Following his Amsterdam visit, Paul travelled to London to see how motorcar development was progressing there. He found that there was interest and even excitement and was proud to see that many of the designs being developed depended upon German, Daimler patents. Early growth in England he discovered, was being hampered by a silly law requiring a man to walk in front of the car with a red flag.

Mercedes Workshop 1912. Paul's first establishment at 15/17 Kanatnaya. Annotated, signed and dated by Paul. Far left is the caretaker, next a 'broker', whose role is not clear, then Paul with cigarette in hand. To <u>his</u> left is his manager and salesman, Herr Etin. Behind are labelled the fitters, engineers and apprentices. Mercedes in Cyrillic is clear on the garage behind.

From the start, Paul's interest had been not just to buy a car but also to start a business. He had enquired whether Mercedes had representation in Russia and in the Odessa region, in particular. It emerged that they were in the process of drawing up agreements in St Petersburg and Moscow and were interested in opening an agency in Odessa. In 1904, the same year in which he graduated, he took delivery of his first Mercedes Simplex car. He enjoyed the stir it caused as he drove through town. Sophia was a slightly unwilling passenger at first but understood Paul's enthusiasm. She realised she had to buy some new clothes more suitable for driving. With air rushing past there could be no large hats. The new car parked very conveniently in the inner courtyard of their Odessa apartment block.

The negotiations regarding the terms of his dealership were challenging. Mercedes were cautious. Paul had no business experience, but he knew the market and had excellent contacts both in Odessa's business world and in the senior Russian administration. Which of the costs and risks were to be with him and which with Mercedes? He agreed that the cost of the premises in Odessa, and of the local technical, administrative and sales staff would be entirely his. The operating capital, comprising mostly the cars for sale, would be shared. He would determine the price at which the vehicles would be sold. How profits would be computed and shared was agreed.

His first combined salesroom and workshop was conveniently close to his Marazlievskaya home, at Kanatnaya Street, 15/17. As demand grew, he agreed with Stuttgart headquarters to expand and transferred the workshop to Peter the Great St, 26, close to St Pauls Cathedral.

He opened a separate showroom at the entrance to the prestigious Ekaterininskaya Square in the centre of town. Early sales had been to fellow, estate-owning German colonists, but the local Russian aristocracy was not to be left behind and ordered luxury models beyond the scope of most colonists. Successful Greek merchants and the top Jewish maklers, members of the first and second merchants guilds, also became clients. Following Paul's lead, second cousin Waldemar Vaatz negotiated to represent two other leading German carmakers, Horch and BMW, respectively. He located his offices in new premises at Sophievskaya, 10, near the harbour. Both enterprises grew steadily. It was competition, but friendly, and the cousins often discussed business together. Tragically both car businesses collapsed immediately when, in 1914 war was declared with Germany.

Paul gained prestige by quickly arranging an alternative agency with French car-maker, De Dion Bouton. He used his old Kanatnaya premises for this business. This arrangement was viable as the French were allies in the war against Germany. But this business also collapsed, soon after, in 1919 when the Revolution reached Odessa. Then Paul had despaired. It seemed the harder he fought the worse things became. He had to get his family and himself out of this mess.

The De-Dion-Bouton Advertisement

***

Whispering interrupts Paul's dreaming of enterprises past. He returns to the present, to darkness and reality. The older Linke boy wants to use the bucket. One of the Uncle Alberts lights a match to allow him to see the way and then kindly blows it out so he can perform without embarrassment. The expected tinkle on tin echoes around the confined space. The sensitive notice the faint characteristic smell. Even in the dark, it is still a public performance. He has set an example, and his younger brother follows. Next, are Isa and Mary, the brothers' older sister. Tamara wants to be an adult and holds on. They continue to wait and, as their eyes get accustomed to the dark, they can see the small splashes of daylight filtering through the woodpile onto the high little window.

Mathilda indicates she needs to 'go,' but as she struggles to stand, there is a sharp bang on the cupboard door and a gruff whisper, *'Die sind da'*[9]

Mathilda's collapses down again, and her needs are forgotten. All listen. They hear the normal sounds of the village, dogs barking, cows lowing, cockerels crowing, wood being chopped, and children playing. Then comes the sound of a truck drawing up. It becomes ominously silent.

A small open troop carrier, with ten heavily armed CheKa militia in the back, very similar to the one that had entered the Grossliebental only a month before, arrives and parks outside the headman's house. The driver jumps out, runs round the front of the truck and opens the door. The commissar steps out wearing a long black leather topcoat with a sabre at his side. As his men clamber out of the rear, he scans the village square, his right hand placed, with elbow out, on the large pistol holster hanging at his front. His men are also all in black leather but in jackets strapped at the waist, black boots and motorbike jodhpurs. They too have pistols, no sabres but each carries a rifle with bayonet attached.

---

[9] They're here.

The commissar orders the headman to summon all villagers into the square. He waits impatiently for them to collect, pacing around his troop carrier and to and fro across the small village square. He is closely watched by the villagers. His men observe the villagers content that they are subdued and appear suitably frightened. When the headman indicates that all except those working in the outer fields are present, the commissar demands,

'Have you seen the Vaatz brothers and their families?'

There is a horrified drawing in of breath, from the hiding adults, as they hear Hilsendeger say, 'Yes,'

It seems obvious he is about to expose them. They gasp together but immediately breathe more freely again when he goes on to explain that the villagers would not let the refugees stay, as they know it is not allowed to harbour refugees. He continues that the refugees had gone off downriver to look for a way to get across and escape to Romania.

The commissar refuses to believe this invention and orders his men to ransack the village and make a thorough search. The CheKa militia stomps through the village houses, knocking over furniture, crashing open doors, breaking china and windows and shooting into the air; all to frighten the villagers. They search under beds, sometimes firing a shot or two into a bed. They thrust their sabres deep into the straw bales being kept dry in the barns. Cupboard doors are slammed open, and as they do this to the cupboard that conceals the families, all jump and hug close, as it feels as if their refuge has been discovered. Sophia holds her hand softly over Isa's mouth to make sure she does not cry out. But Isa cannot breathe, pulls the hand slowly away, stretches up to her mother's ear and promises in a whisper that she will not cry.

When his men find nothing, the commissar becomes angry and desperate.

He says slowly and deliberately, 'I will order my men to shoot you all, one by one, starting with the children, then the women and then the rest, until you tell me where you have hidden those filthy Bourgeoisie.'

Those inside hear this terrible threat and are sure they will now be exposed. The commissar goes further. He orders three of his men to raise their guns and to aim them at a little girl standing at the front of the village group. The girl shrinks in fear and clasps her arms around her mother's legs. The mother lets out a muffled scream and bends to protect her. There is a frightened silence both inside the little store-room and among the huddle of villagers outside. Who can stand up to such an awful threat? Only the scrape of the commissar's boot, as he impatiently taps it on the ground, deciding when to give the order, breaks the silence. He looks at his watch. The villagers crowd closer together. The militia become very tense and alert.

***

A young farmer, moves out of the group of villagers, and nudging his little girl in front, with his hands on her shoulders and ignoring the commissar, takes two steps towards the three gunmen, so he is less than a metre away from the muzzles of their guns.

'Go on then, shoot us if you must,' His little girl looks back and up at him in fear and disbelief, as he goes on, 'but do not call yourselves our comrade revolutionaries and the makers of a new Russia. You are no comrades of ours if you do this terrible thing. You are no revolutionaries if you murder your own kind. Our masters may have underpaid and overworked us, or worse, but they would never shoot us.'

The three men become confused and look questioningly at each other and at their other comrades. They slowly lower their weapons and turn sheepishly towards the commissar for guidance. He is raging inside but dare not give an order that will very probably be disobeyed.

After a pause he says to the headman, while pointedly ignoring the brave young farmer, 'Alright, we will go and search in the direction you have indicated but if we don't find them and come back to discover you are sheltering these enemies of the state we will burn down the whole village and shoot the lot of you.'

The CheKa search party clambers into their vehicle and drives off, the commissar clearly in a furious temper.

***

The little group of refugees has survived once again. But sitting on the floor in that small dark storeroom with his family around him, Paul has lost all heart. He feels the noose closing. Until now, in their flight, the danger has been general. They were just one among many sad, frightened members of the bourgeoisie that the Reds were hunting. But now the CheKa are searching specifically for the Vaatzs, and they know they are somewhere close. How long before someone, either by mistake, or intentionally and naturally to save their own life, reveals where they are?

There are voices and a scraping sound as the headman and friends push the cupboard away. They edge the narrow store-room door open, and inside the light expands from a strip up the wall to a beam of bright sunlight, revealing bags, blankets and eating utensils scattered between the tangle of sitting adult legs on the floor. The children are already half-standing trying not to trip over these legs. They rub their eyes against the light and look around as if newly woken and not quite sure where they are. The adults grunt and complain stiff-jointedly as they rise. Paul and Albert Linke are closest to the door and stoop under its low lintel as they leave first, accompanied by impatient youngsters between their legs. The two men effusively thank Hilsendeger and the two other villagers who had pushed the cupboard aside. The three families emerge from their cell and then from the house into the square.

Most villagers are still gathered there, watching. There is no big cheer at the success of the subterfuge. Most seem happy that their guests have survived and there are many relieved but sad smiles. But there are some, one can tell from their faces who, realising how very close they had been to sharing death with their unwelcome visitors, were thinking, 'What do we do when the CheKa returns?'

The six adults freed from their hiding place, go into the square and thank anyone who will listen - mostly man to man and woman to woman. No one is openly hostile, and the villagers receive the gratitude quietly. Brother-in-law seeks out the brave farmer who risked everything with his inspired speech. His modest reply is that he could have done nothing else. The children go to their village friends and are quickly chatting and comparing their inside and outside experiences. Paul is impressed by how they have adapted to the situation. They are every bit as competent as their elders in playing this macabre game of hide-and-seek with the CheKa.

Once the crowd has dispersed Hilsendeger tells Paul that the villagers have decided that, while the CheKa are still in the area, he and the two Alberts must stay indoors during the day, ready to return quickly into the store-room. Paul accepts the reasonableness of this constraint, but it depresses him, further. The women and children are allowed to share in the life of the village as before.

***

One night they hear shooting and a lot of shouting. Next morning they are told that a family of four had somehow managed to construct a crude raft and had tried to cross the Dniester. The Bolshevik guards had seen and fired at them. Then they were also targeted by the Romanians from the other bank. It appears that more than one of the family were hit. They were last seen drifting down the river toward the sea in the dark. This event finally resigns Paul and Sophia to the fact that trying to escape via Romania is too dangerous to attempt. The CheKa party does not return, and there is news that they have left the area. Paul wonders whether the commissar has assumed that it was his family that had perished on the river.

All routes for escape have now vanished. North and east are the Reds; west is the impassable River the Dniester and south the empty sea. They are trapped and in the awful position of having no plan of escape.

When Paul was worrying or simply planning at home, he would sit at his desk threading his fingers back through his hair in thought and then emerge from the study with it standing on end, as if having just had a terrible fright. The evening following the night-shooting on the River Dniester he appears from the cobbler's house with his hair in this unruly state, having sat desperately trying to work out how to extract his family from the hell they were in. He had been sitting not at a desk but on a farm chair, in front of an unlit fire, with elbows on knees and head in hands. Sophia had learned long ago that if she tried to smooth it down in a motherly fashion, he would get annoyed, push her away, telling her not to fuss. However, experience had also taught her how to avoid this rebuff. She approaches him lovingly from the side, puts her right arm around his waist and smoothens down his hair with her left while kissing him on the cheek, all in one movement. He hardly notices. In fact, he puts his arm around her shoulders and squeezes.

Chapter 16 – Back to Odessa

Amidst this total despair, rumours start, good positive stories but Paul's experience convinces him that they are silly and unbelievable, the result of wishful thinking and *'silly chatter,'* as he calls it. He discounts the tales and gets angry and frustrated when they are repeated to him.

It takes Sophia to persuade him to listen, at least, to the source of the news. This is after she has questioned the farmer concerned and she has been convinced. Making his reservations clear, Paul agrees. The farmer explains he has been given permission to cultivate the land towards Odessa, as the Bolsheviks realise that if they want to eat, they have to allow the farmers to farm. He tells how he had wandered further south than usual to gather-in two cows, which had strayed when he was astonished to come across a newly established White Army guard post. It was less than fifteen versts to the south. The White guards there had confirmed that Denikin had again taken control of Odessa and that all the villages between Odessa and Franzfeld were also free. Perversely, this fantastic news only serves to heighten Paul's frustration, as the Reds are still in control of the Romanian border and of Franzfeld itself and there is no way that he can see to get out past the Red guard posts.

However, a surprisingly simple - if frighteningly dangerous - way is proposed to him. Paul's host has noticed that the Red guards are very confident of their hold on Franzfeld. As a result, they routinely leave their guard-posts at lunchtime, come back to the village to eat and also drink heavily. Most are asleep by early afternoon. Paul's host is convinced it should be possible to slip out of the village during this unofficial 'siesta' time. Paul has a long discussion with Sophia, Albert, Mathilde and the Linkes, and all agree they must take the risk. The risk of staying is possibly even greater, as a nervous villager could expose them at any time.

Their host offers to provide a horse and wagon, and Sophia offers up one of her diamond–bejewelled brooches in payment. She does not begrudge this barter, as she is aware that the villagers are risking their lives in helping them. It is true, also, that the villagers will lessen their risk if they can rid themselves of their uninvited guests.

The following day in the hot early afternoon sun, one of the cobbler's older sons drives the family slowly out of the village, as quietly as he can. He keeps to the grass verge, where possible, to lessen the sound of the horses' hooves and the iron-clad cartwheels. Albert and Mathilde join Paul's family. The Linkes plan to follow the next day, providing all goes well. The village is, indeed, as if dead. While the hard-working German farmers are out in the fields, the Reds are sleeping and snoring like the pigs Paul considers them to be.

Saved from barter. Albert's cufflinks, Sophia's Borel Neuchatel watch, Paul's five rouble gold piece.

The adults, who nervously try to act the part of farmers going to work in their fields, know that all in the cart are at serious risk; the men, including the villager, of being shot, possibly following torture; the women, perhaps, to an even worse fate, and the children of being subjected to harassment, brain-washing and 're-education.'

They pass close to three of the feared revolutionary sailors sprawled, backs against the wall, on a bench outside a village house they will have requisitioned from some poor farmer. One, puffing at a long pipe, pulls his cap down to shade his eyes and watches them pass. Paul nervously returns the stare out of the corner of his own eyes and worries that they have not planned their disguise more carefully – they should at least have carried a rake or two and other farm tools. He will suggest this to the son driving them, for the next planned journey by the Linke family. This assumes the present subterfuge is successful. But no effort is made to stop them. Out of range of the sailors, Paul finds himself sweating and pushes his fingers up through his hair, with both hands, when he realises how close to death they have all been. If just one of those sailors had been a little bit more awake or a tiny bit curious and had stood up and called for them to stop that would have been the end. They wouldn't pass as peasants under close interrogation.

Once outside the village, the fugitives breathe more easily. However, they remain nervous as they approach the Red guard-box, for until reaching it they cannot be sure whether there is anyone inside. There is not. Just three unwashed tea glasses in their holders, beside an unlit samovar and a stool on which lies the Bolshevik newspaper *The Fight*, held down by a stone. They relax further but save their celebrations until they are two versts further on, and out of sight of the guard post when the cobbler's son drops them off to return to Franzfeld. Sophia and Mathilde stand, hug and sob, and the girls cry with them. The men remind them they are still not quite home yet and must walk further. It takes another hour's walk along the dykes to reach the Denikin Army guard post. They see Russian red, white and blue flag flying from a small blockhouse and increase their pace.

A loud shout of *'Stoyi!'* (Russian, 'stop!') shatters the sighs and mutterings of relief as they approach the guard house.

Two guards rush from the post with rifles held level, the bayonets pointed directly at Albert and Paul's midriffs. The two tentatively raise their hands.

But Sophia is cross, holds her hands round Isa and Tamara's shoulders. 'Can't you see you're frightening the children? We're running for our lives, and you point your nasty guns at us?'

The soldiers' look at each other and again at Sophia, and lower their weapons with embarrassment, and there are apologies, but also explanations.

'We have to be careful. There are Reds everywhere.'

The exhausted escapees then receive a warm welcome. Paul and Albert are questioned closely about their experience, as the information they can provide, of the numbers and location of the enemy, is essential intelligence. From the busy Morse rat-tat-tapping of the operator in the next room, it seems that this intelligence is already being telegraphed to headquarters. They are poured tea from the small samovar that is bubbling gently away at the back of the guardroom. Paul notices the folded newspaper on the table and finds it somehow ironic how similar the Red and White guard posts are. He informs the guards that, if all goes to plan, there will be another party arriving tomorrow and that they do not need to be quite so cautious. Albert Linke confirms, later, that he did not have to put up his hands but was greeted warmly when his family arrived.

The bedraggled and tired Vaatz and Linke families are horrified at what they encounter as they pass from Franzfeld through Alexanderhilf to Grossliebental. These villages and, as they discover soon after, the others like Kleinliebental and the seaside settlement of Lustdorf, that had all resisted the Bolsheviks, are badly destroyed. There have been fires, doors and windows have been smashed in. The villagers are living in the shells of their houses or in ramshackle shelters; they have had to construct from the ruins. The fugitives see the results of the plunder, destruction and murder of innocent German colonists and Ukrainian farmers, who had merely been trying to save their property and their lives.

In Grossliebental and Kleinliebental the Reds had murdered over forty villagers out of revenge[10]. These had been hurriedly buried in a shallow grave. Before moving on the Vaatzs and Linkes together, attend their re-burial by Pastor Koch with a proper Christian service. He, poor man, just because he was a pastor, was later sent to Siberia with his family. The father of Sophia's cousin, Wilhelm, who had helped the family escape Odessa, was shot with those in Grossliebental but Wilhelm himself and his wife had managed to survive. The destruction and death wreaked would have been even higher had the Reds not been threatened by the advance of Denikin's forces upon Odessa. This lead to them terminating their punitive activities and rushing back to assist in the defence of the town. They arrived too late to have any real effect.

Paul and Sophia stay on a few days in Grossliebental to be with her mother. Her house has some smashed windows, but it has not been fired like many of the others. The Reds concentrated their destruction on the homes of those they thought had contributed to the peasant's revolt. In spite of the death and damage, her mother is still determined to remain. She says she is too old to travel and that, in any case, she has now experienced, first hand, that the Reds do not bother with an old village woman. Paul persuades the girls that the kindest thing to do is to leave Maxi with Oma. She loves the dog and there is no way that the family would be able to take him with them when they go to Germany. So Maxi also experiences hugs and tears as the family departs. Although Sophia accepts that is probably true that her mother will not be persecuted by the Bolsheviks, she still has a pit in her stomach at the realisation that this is the last time she will see her strong, brave Mama. She hugs her fiercely as they say their goodbyes.

On their way back, further along the route they had fled in the opposite direction some eight weeks ago, they call on Mrs Van Dych. They want to know how she has coped and must arrange for the return of their furniture and effects to the apartment in Odessa. She is relieved and pleased to see them but recounts how the CheKa had terrorised the town. They had taken thousands to their torture building in Ekaterininskaya Square and routinely executed them with a shot in the back of the neck. This included all military officers,

---

[10]. The death toll in three of the villages around Odessa was later given as: Grossliebental 20, Kleinliebental 22, Selz 87, Worms 12.

many in the church, property owners, bankers, factory and business owners and anyone who they considered to be an enemy of Communism.

Mrs Van Dych tells them that during their absence from Odessa, the Red's had proclaimed the *Glorious Acquisition of the Russian Proletarian Revolution* – this decreed the *socialisation* of women. All the Red newspapers announced - and Paul is sorry that he did not keep a copy of the notice - that females between eighteen and forty had been *socialised*. This proclaimed that it was allowed to have sex with any woman, married or not, to live with them as long as they wished and to discard them at will. Paul sees this as a Bolshevik conspiracy to destroy the Russian Christian nation. And he is frustrated and angry that the world stands by and watches, says nothing and does nothing.

Next, with a sad and apologetic look on her face and murmuring condolences, Mrs Van Dych gives Paul the 17 July 1919 issue of the Bolshevik newspaper *Borjba,* printed on yellow packing paper. Paul accepts it with a well-justified trepidation, for marked in purple, indelible pencil he sees that brother Carl is listed as having been executed for the 'crime' of being a *property-owner and counter-revolutionary*. He had, in spite of the warning of friends, stayed in his Odessa house. Paul realises that this death was less than a month ago, while he and Sophia were still stuck in Franzfeld.

Mrs Van Dych presents Paul with a final piece of paper. He unfolds it carefully to discover that it is a *Trebuetsya (*Wanted) notice offering a reward of fifty thousand Roubles for information leading to his arrest. He is described as '*Property Owner and Representative of Mercedes in Odessa.*' He realises that this sum is a very tempting incentive for workers to expose their bosses, as it is more than many might earn in a whole year. Further thoughts pass through Paul's mind when digesting the size of the reward. First, he mentally blesses and thanks the many villagers who had risked their lives for his family and ignored the considerable sum offered. Second, he recalls that in 1915 he had invested a very similar amount in Tsarist bonds to support the war effort against the Germans and that these bonds must now be worthless.

In spite of the many dangers and real hardships they have suffered, Paul and Sophia agree it had been a wise decision to flee to the German villages and then to travel yet further west to escape the Liebental massacres. Mrs Van Dych has another piece of news that makes this apparently obvious conclusion a little less certain. This is that, had they managed to survive only a few days in Grossliebental, rather than flee to Franzfeld, they would have been safe and spared the several nasty experiences they had suffered there. Denikin marched back into Odessa and the surrounding villages only ten days after the family had left. Paul consoles himself that he and his family are still alive. No one can say whether they would have survived or whether he might have been added to the over forty male villagers murdered in the massacres, had they stayed behind.

The family arrives back at Marazlievskaya 14b at the end of August 1919. Their beautiful modern apartment is now a rubbish tip. Worse, slogans are written all over the walls: *Bugger off white bourgeois riffraff; bloodsucking bastards; see you soon, then you will hang*. Piles of waste and rubbish are everywhere on the floors, in the fireplaces, in the bath, and faeces on the walls. The telephone has been pulled out and is gone.

Tamara notices this especially as she was proud she had learned how to answer the phone.

'Odessa 42-68,' she would say in a firm voice, 'Tamara Vaatz speaking.'

And if Mama and Paper were out she would carefully note down any message on the pad beside the phone. The little polished walnut side table with its gilded frets, on which it had stood, was now lying on its side with a broken leg. It made her sad. She would need to learn a new number in a new home in Germany but she would never forget this one.

At every step they take, their shoes crunch on broken glass and china. They inspect the soles of their shoes and try to scrape off the shards, to get rid of the persistent scrunching. Almost worse is what they can't see. The ammoniac smell of urine and faeces mixed with yet further unsavoury aromas, including stale alcohol, make Sophia want to retch. They cannot stay in the apartment and certainly not with their children who, as Paul remarks, again need to be going to school.

Paul and Sophia agree they need to restore everything to its former condition as quickly as they can, replace all the fittings and furniture, and then sell the flat complete with its contents. They will then find a way to emigrate to Germany. In the meantime, Albert and Mathilda are happy to squeeze the family into their temporary accommodation in the German Quarter close to St Paul's Evangelical Cathedral. Paul works hard to achieve the challenging task of restoration as quickly as is feasible using a combination of firm persuasion and generous payments.

While Paul was trapped in Franzfeld, the *Zentralkomitees des Verbandes der deutschen Kolonisten im Schwarzmeergebiet* (Central Committee of German Colonists in the Black Sea region,) a self-defence force under the command of Major General Schöll had been formed in Odessa. In agreement with the Liebental group of village colonies, conscription for men of thirty-six and thirty-seven, and a levy to cover the costs of the force was introduced. Brother Albert is a keen supporter but, although Paul pays his dues and reads their newsletter, *Die Vereinsbote* (Literally, 'Club offering.' Title of the newsletter) he is not at all optimistic as to what they can achieve.

Chapter 17– At Karlovka

Tamara is feeling sorry for herself. August has just ended, but it is still hot. They are squeezed in with Uncle Albert and Aunty Tilla and have almost no toys or books, and she can tell Papa is very stressed. She is happy to be back in lovely, beautiful Odessa but the Bolsheviks have made their home nasty and dirty, and although Papa was getting it fixed, it was only to sell it. He and Mama wanted to run away again. To Germany this time where everyone spoke German. She and Isa had never been keen on speaking German. Only Oma used to insist that they must. Tamara cries to herself when she remembers that Oma has decided not to come with them. She recalls how in a normal year they would have been in Karlovka in summer and how, just two years ago in 1917, they had gone a little earlier than usual to Uncle Albert's estate.

Tamara tells – Summer June 1917

We were excited. We were on our way to see Onkel (Uncle) Albert and Tante (Aunty) Tilla who were expecting us for our usual summer visit. The journey to the estate was a great adventure, as we otherwise never travelled by train. We kissed Mama and Papa good-bye in the flat and returned their waves as they stood on the balcony waving to us. In previous years we had gone to the station by horse and carriage but this year Papa arranged for his chauffeur to take us by car.

At the station porters carried Mademoiselle's and our luggage to the train. She presented our tickets and we were shown to our carriage and the luggage loaded. We had two two-berth compartments between us. Mademoiselle opened the connecting door. Then Isa and I argued over who was to have the top bunk. We stopped when Mademoiselle threatened that we could both have a top bunk but one would be with her. We settled with scissor stone and Isa got the top bunk on the condition that the next time it would be my turn. I didn't know then that there would not be a 'next time.' Going by train was great fun.

Mademoiselle Voutaz came with us as Papa insisted that our lessons continued while we were away from home. Apart from French, Mademoiselle Voutaz taught us other subjects, including history, geography, maths and some English. She was also supposed to teach us manners. It was her job to make sure we sat straight and not put our elbows on the table. Papa expected her to bang our elbows when we forgot. She did so but very gently. We both quite liked Mademoiselle Voutaz. She was fair and tried to be strict, but we soon realised that her job depended upon her getting on well with us and I am ashamed that we were sometimes more cheeky than we should have been.

The attendant knocked politely and asked what we wanted for supper. I looked at the menu and immediately suggested to Isa that we should have Pampushki. I knew we would get them again in Karlovka. It didn't matter, it was one of our favourites. They are fried potato dumplings filled with cheese and herbs. Mademoiselle decided to eat French and chose Filet Mignon together with a glass of red wine. We had fresh orange. We enjoyed sitting at our private little fold-down table by the window and being served separately from Mademoiselle; she eating from her own little table. We could then hold our secret discussions. We finished with warm milk with honey to help us sleep.

Mademoiselle did not have to tell us to get changed into our night-dresses and get to bed. We wanted to go. She kissed us each on the forehead and wished us good night, telling us not to chat for too long. She closed the joining door but left it slightly ajar. This was so she could leave her light on and read while we were sleeping. May be she also wanted some privacy for changing.

We did whisper together for a while, planning what we would do and what we would say to Aunty Tilla but we were tired and it was special to snuggle under the duvets and to be lulled to sleep by the regular rumble of the rails. Before whispering good-night to each other, I said a little prayer for Isa that Mama had taught me:

> *Ich bin klein*
> *Mein Herz ist rein*
> *Soll niemand drin wohnen*
> *Als Jesus allein.*[11]

The bright morning sun shining in through the east-facing window woke me early. We had forgotten to pull down the blind. Isa was still asleep so I plumped up and doubled my pillows to see out while still lying down. I imagined the bears and the wolves in winter. I savoured the rattle of the rails, and dreamily watched the steam, smoke and sometimes soot blowing past the windows. Isa and Mademoiselle soon also woke and she ordered breakfast, which we ate while still in our night dresses. We all had Syrniki (cottage cheese pancakes) with sour cream and raspberry jam, together with lemon tea.

Once we had washed in our private little sink, and dressed, we watched the scenery flashing past. There were fields and forests, in some places very wild with no buildings or people in sight. In others peasants were busy looking after sheep or cattle or collecting vegetables from the fields. Mademoiselle insisted we must not lean out of the windows as she said the soot would dirty our dresses, and it was dangerous, we would get our heads knocked off. We couldn't see how and what damage could air rushing through our hair do? So when she was sat reading in her own compartment we would quickly poke our heads out and enjoy the wind rushing past. We waved at anyone we saw and laughed happily when they waved back. Mademoiselle tut-tutted and said it was all most unladylike.

Soon after leaving *Amanya*, the steward knocked on the compartment door and reminded us that the next station was ours. As we had already packed our cases he carried them to the carriage door. We waited by the door while Mademoiselle continued to sit on her bed reading until the train slowed for *Kameni-Most* (Stone

---

[11] I am small, My heart is pure, No one shall enter, Except Jesus alone.

Bridge) when she packed her book away and waited beside us and the luggage. We were impatient to get out.

I leant out of the carriage door window as the train slowed into the station to the sound of squealing brakes. I sensed that behind me Mademoiselle wanted to tell me to be careful but she didn't. Uncle Albert's coach driver in his green livery, was waiting on the platform, and I waved. It was a very small station, nothing like Odessa with a very small platform, shorter than the train but we were all right, our carriage door finished in a good place. Both Isa and I jumped out not wanting any help but Mademoiselle accepted assistance of the coachman and descended very gracefully. He carried two cases as he showed us to the landau drawn by a fine black horse. He helped us in and then had to return to the platform to collect two more cases.

We were soon trotting out of the little town and for two kilometres or so drove to the left of the railway. We turned sharply right over a rather bumpy and steep railway crossing. Mademoiselle stretched her arms wide, holding both sides of the carriage to steady herself. The farm lane we entered was rocky and was dusty because of the dry weather. We passed fields of tall, almost ripened corn and were welcomed by endless rows of even taller sunflowers nodding at us in the breeze. Sometimes the lane got so narrow that the flowers hung into the carriage. We were pushing through a sea of gold. They were not yet quite ripe, but I hoped that we could find some seeded flower heads when we got to the farm. Then Isa and I could practice eating the *zemechki* (Sunflower seeds) like the peasants, putting a small handful of the seeds in our mouth, shelling them one by one, with our teeth and then spitting out the husks into a little pile. We could only do this when Mademoiselle was not watching.

Mademoiselle settled herself with her back to the coachman, holding a lacy white umbrella and attempting to read in spite of the jolting carriage. We sat opposite with two smaller discarded sun umbrellas lying on the seat beside us. She had tried to persuade us to use them. But we quickly became bored and, in spite of her protests, laid them aside as our skin didn't need protecting.

We arrived at the Frank farm but, as we did not know them well and the track took us around the edge of their estate, and not past the main house, we did not stop. At the Roemmich estate, a few fields further on, the track took us right through their main yard. It would have been impolite not to say 'Hello.' In any case, we liked them and we were related. Great Aunt Marie being married to Great Uncle Heinrich Roemmich. They were happy to see us and tried to persuade us to stay, but we were still only halfway on our coach ride and had to get on. So we accepted a quick, iced lemonade while sitting in the shade of the sweet chestnut tree at the edge of the yard. The two horses were snuffling noisily and enjoying their drink at the trough close by. While he didn't snuffle, the coachman was obviously also content, sipping his cold beer sitting sideways, high up on his coach seat.

Soon after leaving the Roemmich estate we came to the main road that went north from Odessa towards Kiev. We turned right and south. This road was wider but, although it had once been surfaced, was not any smoother. In fact, it had deeper pot-holes than the farm lanes. Our coachman had to weave a path between them. We met our first traffic; carts loaded with hay, one with a peasant girl and boy sitting on top, to whom we waved and shouted as we passed. A stage-coach went by, full of passengers and with luggage loaded on top. We questioned Mademoiselle as to whether they were going to Kiev. She replied it was possible but unlikely as most people now went by train because it was far more comfortable and much quicker.

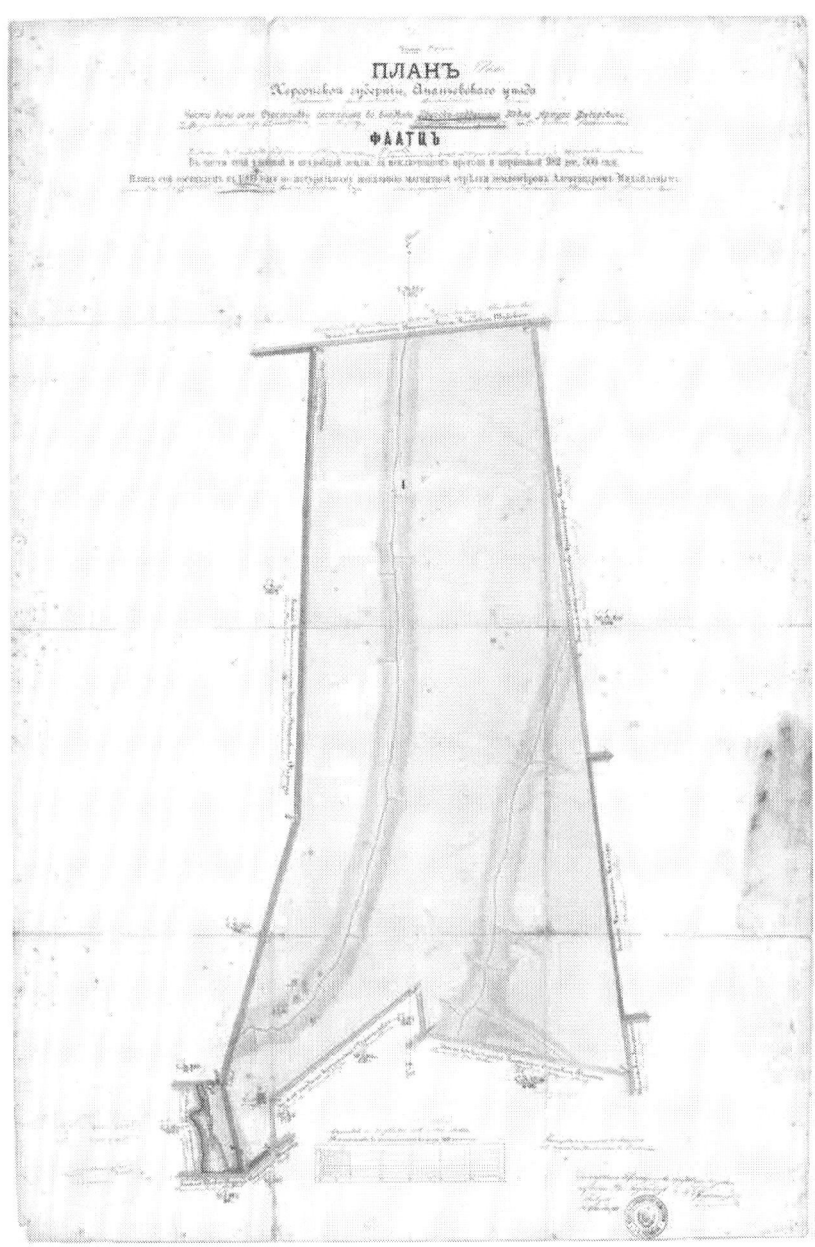

Paul's Schastlivka estate. The dark line to the left is the Odessa – Kiev road. The owners of the properties surrounding the estate are clearly marked. Brother Carl's lies to the West of the road.

We reached the Schastlivka estate, previously owned by Grandfather Friedrich Vaatz whom I couldn't remember ever having met. He must have died before I was born, or when I was very young. Papa's estate bordered the road to the left, as we drove, for at least five kilometres. Papa, Uncle Albert and Uncle Carl were all born there, and each had inherited a share.

I wondered why we had never been to Papa's estate. Perhaps he did visit, but if so, he never took us. Mama had told me that an estate manager looked after the farm and that Uncle Carl kept an eye on things. Further south, another part of the old estate was now owned by grandmother Caroline. We didn't see her nearly as much as Mama's mother, who we called Oma and whose real name was Friederike. Grandmother Caroline sometimes came to see us, though, when we were at Karlovka and Mama and Papa came to visit there.

As we got closer to Karlovka, the countryside became more rolling and wooded, and there were water meadows with grazing sheep and cows. Peasants were working in the fields. We became excited when we saw a mother bear and cub and told the coachman to slow. We watched them splashing and playing at the edge of the forest in the shallows of the River Bakshala. This was the same meandering river that flowed through Uncle Albert's estate, and that widened out into several large lakes along its length.

We started to compete as to who would be the first to see the conical tower of Uncle's farmhouse above the forest trees. Mademoiselle got concerned and told us off when we stood up in the rocking carriage to get a better view. I'm afraid I made her really cross when I tried to stand on my seat to win the competition. I sheepishly had to get down and while I was sulking Isa shrieked that she had seen the tower.

We surreptitiously loosened our summer shoes and pushed down our white ankle socks with the opposite foot, making sure our governess did not notice. I had shared my plan with Isa.

Karlovka. Tower. Mathilde, the governess, Tamara and Isa stand in front.

We turned left on to the estate and into the shade of its trees. The surface became smoother. Half a kilometre further we rolled right, into the drive and yard of the main house. This was surfaced with fine pebble gravel and crunched under the carriage wheels. Mademoiselle started to worry at what time we were expected and whether they would be ready to welcome us. As the coach entered the house yard, she was too busy checking whether anyone was waiting for us, and we surreptitiously slipped off our shoes and socks. Our coachman stood up, straightened his green livery and called out loudly that we had arrived. Mademoiselle put her hands to her ears.

A servant appeared immediately and hurried to open the carriage door and to help Mademoiselle down. But we jumped out first, under Mademoiselle's arms, in our bare feet, and ran screaming into the garden, hobbling quickly over the gravel and then on to the soft grass, enjoying its feel between our toes. We hid in the surrounding bushes. Mademoiselle held up her hands in confusion but then, stepped down, walked sedately towards the house, turned, looked towards our hiding place, tapped her knuckles on the marble top of the garden table and shouted, but genteelly, in French.

'Girls, Tamara, Isa, come out at once. Change and get ready for your lessons.'

We remained hidden, giggled silently, and peeped at her through the leaves. Our saviour Tante Tilla emerged, came down the stone steps, patted Mademoiselle kindly on the arm and also in French, suggested that the girls could catch up with their lessons later and that she should rest and join her in the garden, with cake and a glass of tea. All this, before we two had even said hello to our aunt and uncle. So much for our manners. We crept among the fruit bushes picking and swallowing raspberries, red currants and other fruit. We were a little too late for the strawberries, but we did discover a few hidden under the leaves.

Then Aunty called, 'All right girls you can come out now and have a piece of cake but be sure you apologise properly to Mademoiselle, first.'

The promise of cake was an effective bribe. We emerged from hiding, apologised in our best French and were then allowed to feast greedily on the treat of fresh *Apfelstrudel* and *Schlagsahne* (Whipped cream.) We also remembered to say 'Hello' politely to Tante Tilla and to thank her for the tea treat. If we had come later in the year, as usual, we would have been given *Zwetschgentorte (*Plum tart) *und Schlagsahne,* that was my favourite. I loved the blend of sourness and sweet smoothness on my tongue. Then we had to change, and very soon we were exploring the garden again.

***

On 6th June, after we had been at Karlovka for just over two weeks, I received a pretty postcard from Mama with a little girl holding a dachshund (It could have been our Max) in her arms:

> Dear Tamarochka[12],
>
> There was a big congress of landowners here in Odessa this week. Many private landowners and even more peasants attended. All were worried both about the war and now the terrible revolution in St Petersburg. Uncle can read all about it the newspaper where it is described in detail. I would so much like to visit you my dear children, but I can't. So if uncle is not coming to town soon, do not wait for him. Just come back with Mademoiselle. Today I supervised the thorough cleaning of the whole apartment. Tamarik, don't forget your promise to Mama not to offend Mademoiselle and not to be rude to her. You need to be careful and watch your manners.
>
> Many, many kisses to both my darling daughters.
>
> Mama.

Mademoiselle must have complained about us jumping out of the carriage in front of her. A bit mean.

***

We loved visiting the cook-house and tasting the delicious Borsht made for the workers and the dark black rye bread, baked fresh

---

[12] Tamarochka and Tamarik are diminutives of Tamara. Among family and friends the Russians rarely seem to use the given-name.

every day. After dark, the workmen sang their traditional Russian songs. By then, we would have usually been made to go to bed, but their melodic singing still made me happy.

Like on other German-owned estates, our uncle's house was built of stone. The colonists wanted to be sure their homes could not burn down. It was a solid square, just a single living story but standing on a pedestal with twenty steps up to the front door that gave it grandeur and provided a semi-basement for storage.

In summer we sat and had our meals by one of the outer walls, so we had a view. Deciding on which side depended upon whether we were seeking sun or shade. In front of the main door was a large garden with flower-beds, mature trees for shade and shelter from the wind and fruit trees and berry bushes. A pair of poplar trees guarded the front door. The house had a tall steeple-pointed tower at its south-west corner with a weather vane on top — just a simple arrow pointing the direction of the wind. There was no proper room at the top of the tower, but a circular stone stairway led to a landing where we could look out over the farm. This vantage point was the centre for many of our imagined adventures.

We had so much to do, from playing with our dolls and other toys, of which we had a second set waiting for us in our Karlovka nursery, to exploring the estate, the river, the fields and woods and its barns and buildings. While we did play with our dolls outside and take them for walks in their prams, carefully sheltering them from the sun, they were usually reserved for when the storms came. We then liked to bring them on to the veranda to listen with us to the rain drumming on the glass roof and splashing heavily on to the drive. We put our hands out under the eves and felt it hard on our palms. The rain made a distinctive smell as it hit the dry summer dust.

We would tell our dolls not to be frightened of the thunder and counted, 'One, two, three......,'

We counted from when the lightning flashed until the thunder rumbled, to work out how far away the lightning was. This was something Uncle had taught us, and we got a little frightened, in spite of what we told our dolls, as the count got shorter and shorter. And it is true when both come together the lightning is really close.

Making *Gogl-Mogl*[13] had become a custom with us whenever we sat on the veranda watching the storm with our dolls. We went to the kitchen and begged a large egg each and a jar of sugar. We each cracked an egg and separated the egg yolk into a mug. To this, we added a few teaspoons of sugar and then whisked the mix as hard as we could. The challenge was to see who could produce the whitest mixture. The more vigorously and the longer we stirred, the whiter our mix became. We learned that ensuring no egg white got into the mug with the yolk was vital to getting the whitest mix. Aunty or Mademoiselle usually had to act as judge - a judgement that was always questioned by the looser. It was also a challenge to see who would give up first and just eat up the sweet mix.

Even better than making Gogl-Mogl in a storm, was making ice-cream on a hot, hot Summer's day. The first bit was the most exciting. Isa and I begged to be allowed to go with Fadeya, the man-servant who does the heavy work, to the ice-house. This was on the left side of the yard behind the main house. Isa and I carried the wooden bucket between us, while Fadeya had an ice axe and shovel. We arrived at the heavy wooden door framed by a white limestone arched entranceway. This gave entry into a low earth and grass-covered mound, not much higher than the door, itself. But we knew it was bigger inside. Fadeya took a big iron key from his apron front pocket and turned it in the lock. The cold air hit our faces as the door creaked open. Stone steps disappeared steeply down into the dark. We couldn't see the bottom.

We took two candles, in their holders, from our bucket and Fadeya opened his tin box of matches and managed to light both candles with a single match, as Isa and I each protected our flame from the draft. The three of us edged carefully down into the dark on the wet stone steps. Fadeya went a little ahead, in the middle. He held the bucket, with his tools inside, in his left hand. With his right, he steadied himself on the low arched ceiling. Isa was on his right where she could hold onto the iron handrail. I had to descend, using

---

[13] A traditional Jewish desert eaten 'as is' or with a variety of alternative additions; also the foundation of many cake mixes.

just the damp wall on the left to keep my balance. We both held our candles forward and high, to see as far down into the dark as possible.

Twelve steps down we came to a small ledge and Fadeya told us to stop and be careful. He slipped over the edge on his front then stood facing us with the ledge halfway up his chest. He took our candles and placed one right, and one left in little niches specially cut into the wall. He then lifted us both down on to the floor of ice. We shuffled with our feet to help him push aside the layer of straw so he could hack out lumps of ice. These were about the size of a fist, and we shovelled them into the wooden bucket. High above us in the centre of the dark ceiling, I could see a glimmer of light. This was from the air hole that appeared, outside, as a little chimney poking through the grass covering the top of the ice-house. We had been told that when the ice-house was full, the depth of ice was equal to the height of four men. In the winter the ice was sawn, from the lakes on the estate. It usually lasted the full year in the ice-house. There was a long ladder against the opposite wall. This was needed when the ice level got much lower than when we visited.

Once the bucket was full, Fadeya lifted us back onto the ledge and handed us each our candle. He placed his tools on top of the ice in the bucket and lifted that on to the ledge. He then clambered up himself. Isa and I showed the way up again with our candles. As Fadeya pushed open the door, we were flooded in sunlight and warmth. The candles blew out in the draft. I realised how cold I was and only then started to shiver. But this soon stopped as we warmed-up on our walk back to the house. We each took a tool off the top of the bucket and walked back, unlit candle in one hand and ice tool in the other.

We were welcomed into the kitchen as if we had just conquered Everest.

'Was it cold, was it steep, was it dark, were there any snakes?'

One or two of the maids thought us very brave to have gone down there. The ice-cream machine stood ready and open at the end of the kitchen table. The outside was made of wood with iron bands, rather like our ice bucket. In the middle was a metal pot. We helped to crush the ice into small pieces and fed it into the space between the metal pot and wooden container. A maid added some salt into the ice - she said to, make the ice colder. I asked her how, but she had no answer and shrugged. (I must remember to ask Papa.) The sweet ice-cream mix was ready, so we poured it into the centre chamber and closed it up. The lid had a stirrer underneath and a handle on top. All other work in the kitchen had stopped with it seemed everyone helping and advising us what to do.

Next began the hard work. I begged the first stir and began with too much enthusiasm and was advised to be gentler, 'Go slow.' Isa got impatient and pushed me aside but did not last very long either, so one of the maids took over, showing us how to do it- slowly and gently. We sat and watched. There were a few tastings and testings on the way, and when all agreed the ice cream was ready, we helped to spoon it into small glasses and arranged fresh raspberries on top. We two then proudly carried the results of our hard work to present to the grown-ups sitting on the terrace. The head maid followed a little behind, to ensure nothing went wrong. Our ice-cream making adventure was a great success.

Out in the open, we climbed trees, ate all the fruit we wanted and dug little holes to store it in. One day we returned to our hidden stores, I squealed when I found an ugly, fat, spotted toad sitting there. Brave little sister showed off and picked it up, held it in the palm of her left hand and pretended to stroke and then kiss it. She waved her right hand over it, saying 'abracadabra' and wished it to turn into a handsome prince. I shook my head and gave her a grown-up look that said, stupid little girl. For once she didn't put her tongue out but just gave me a shrug meaning, magic doesn't work every time, and set it down to crawl away under the leaves.

The workers in the fields were all polite and welcoming and worried and cautioned us if we climbed too high in the barn or got too close to working machinery. But they let us sit on a horse or ride on the top of the hay cart when it was being brought in. I remembered the noise of the steam-driven thresher and the mixed smell of the diesel and the dust. A favourite game was to slide down the chute of the machine when it was not working. One day I ended up in a wet, smelly cow-pat and made the mess worse trying to clean it up. In desperation, we went to a workman's house, and his wife washed and ironed my things while Isa and I sat, me half-naked, swinging our legs in the sun on the bench.

Another day we went to play with Dancia, the cook's daughter, while her mother was busy in the big house. Like others in the estate village, her home had whitewashed mud-brick walls and a thatched roof. The best room had a large bed with many pillows with pretty cross-stitch embroidery in red and blue. In another room, the tile-covered stove took up half the space. It was used both for cooking and to sleep on in winter There was a four rung wooden ladder to climb on top and curtains hung from the ceiling to keep out the draft..

While we were playing, I noticed our coloured pencils that had been missing, lying in a corner on the floor. Without a word, when Dancia wasn't looking, we just picked them up and took them home. As I got older, I realised what a mean thing that was to have done. For, if our cook had known, she would have been frightened of losing her job, accused of stealing. Fortunately, nothing happened.

By the evening, we were invariably tired and did not object to going to bed. Before that, getting the water to the right temperature for the bath was always a procedure with alternating cries of, 'too cold' and 'you're scolding me!' Evenings were atmospheric. In town, we had got used to our bright electric lights, but here in the country, although the house was as modern as it could be, there was still no running water or electricity. So we experienced the light and shadows and smell of oil lamps and flickering candles as we prepared for bed.

Two or three times during our stay we used to go with Tante Tilla, the maid and sometime Mademoiselle Voutaz to the nearest little town of Domanyok for shopping. That was interesting and fun as we invariably were bought a little treat, whether sweets or a toy.

On one such trip we had a terrible shock. Our carriage drove past a dead man tied to a post. He was all black and had obviously been murdered by lighting fire round him. Mademoiselle tried to stop us looking, but it was too late and although it was horrible and cruel, he could not hurt us. In town Tante asked what had happened.

Apparently he was discovered stealing horses, and the local *Mushiks* (peasants) had exacted their own kind of justice. They were poor and the few horses they owned were vital to their livelihood. On the return journey Isa and I stared again at the strange and horrible black statue, accompanied by Mademoiselle's worried murmurings, as to what it might do to our sleep.

Sometimes Mama and Papa would come and visit and also other aunts, uncles and cousins, especially Uncle Albert Linke with Aunt Nellie and their children, Mary, Fred and Buba came. When there were visitors, there would be a special meal, probably prepared in the summer kitchen and served outside on the terrace. Much grown-up talk took place with Papa asking silly questions as to whether we had behaved and been studious in our lessons. Tante Tilla always answered these enquiries in the affirmative. We then went off with our cousins and explored the farm with them.

On Karlovka Steps. Back row Cornelia and Albert Linke. Left below them, Governess Mlle Voutaz. Below again, Mary and Buba Linke. In front Tamara, Isa, Fred Linke. Back right Sophia. Girl below, a mystery.

***

One day, after we had asked too many questions, Aunty Tilla sat us down and explained how the farm worked. Buyers came from both east and west including, England, Loz, and Moscow. The bargaining was done by Jewish *maklers* (brokers.) Their strange looks fascinated us with their long black caftans, tall hats or skull caps and *payos* (curls) hanging down both sides of their face. Muslim buyers, some in turbans and long white *thawbs* came from the Caucuses mainly to buy rams. To me, when they walked, they seemed to float along as if they have wheels rather than feet. Like other buyers, they often spent the night. They brought their prayer mats and were given rooms facing east.

Women did the sheep shearing, but we never saw that as it happened in spring before we arrived. The wool was then packed into big sacks and loaded on to carts for transport to the station and from there to Odessa harbour. Sunflowers, maize, wheat, rye and barley were all grown and sold to buyers, many of whom stayed overnight. The grain travelled by cart to Vosnessensk on the River Bug and from there by ship to Nikolayev on the Bug - Black Sea estuary.

Summer, when we usually visited, was a hectic time. A herd of 3,000 Merino sheep was kept on an estate of 7,550 morgen (4,718 acres). Over a hundred working and Anglo-Arabian riding horses were bred. The riding horses were mainly sold to the Tsar's army. The three hundred pigs were for the meat and sausages needed to help feed the four hundred workers. There were also chickens, ducks and geese. Nine dogs and twice as many cats, it seemed, added to the list of farm animals. As it started to get dark, all received a saucer of milk.

The workers lived in white lime-washed wood and mud-brick houses. There were many low wooden barns and other farm buildings for housing the animals, storing corn and hay and the farm machinery. This machinery was mostly driven by steam. However, horses were still important. A dam had been built in the river to ensure a secure supply of water. But there was no running water and hand - and horse-drawn water carts of all sizes were scattered around the various yards to ensure it was available for both animals and people.

The estate had its own church and graveyard. We would go and look at the headstones of earlier Vaatzs and ask Tante Tilla what she remembered about them.

Being at the cemetery reminded Aunty of a sad story. Long ago she and Uncle Albert had been invited to the wedding of a Susana Kraus in Petrivka, north of Karlovka. They and many other guests had collected at the same *Kameni-Most* station where Uncle Albert's carriage had come to collect us for our summer holiday. But this was a winter wedding and the guests were excited to be making the last leg of their journey by sledge. Just as they were all were properly wrapped up and ready to set off, a cousin arrived with unbelievably sad news. The wife of Susana's brother had died in the night. They thought it was probably of diphtheria as she had complained of a sore throat. A doctor did arrive but because of the snow and the considerable distance he had to travel, he was much too late. The cousin persuaded the guests still to come but for a funeral rather than a wedding. The wedding did happen but almost a year later.

Red beard. Griffin, the red bearded groom with stallion.
Karlovka view. House and outbuildings. River and lakes in valley to the right.

Karlovka yard. The main entrance is between two poplars. The visible stairs are at the back entrance and lead to little house to right, which is the summer kitchen. Left is the cowshed. Horses are behind the camera. The water carts are essential as there is no running water.

Chapter 18 – Baba Yaga

Paul is busy organising the restoration and for the sale of their apartment. At the same time he is desperately searching for news on how and when they might be able to escape from Odessa. So Sophia sees her primary task as that of caring for and keeping her two girls happy. She remembers the bulrushes that she had asked Paul to pick on that journey to Franzfeld and fishes them out of the bag in which she had stored them. The plan she proposes to Tamara and Isa is that they turn the bulrushes into stick puppets, and she explains how. They need no persuading and quickly decide that their first play will be one of the Baba Yaga[14] stories. They will need bits of paper and cloth to dress them, and Sophia provides a little precious flour to make a paste for sticking. The girls have brought a small artists travelling box of paints with them.

They immediately start planning, designing and searching for the bits and pieces they need. Baba Yaga, the wicked witch, is their first creation. She is given evil white shirt-button eyes with black seed pupils, a hooked nose fashioned from a large acacia bush thorn and sharp teeth of white wheat. She is all in black and is provided with the mortar and pestle in which Russian witches traditionally travel. The mortar is a broken half-cup. This allows Baba Yaga to appear to be sitting inside as she flies across the stage. The cup is painted black with a mixture of soot and wet flour. Now for the other characters. The heroine of the tale, the beautiful little Vasilia has a

---

[14] Baba Yaga is the wicked witch at the centre of many Russian fairy tales.

perfect white face with blue-bead eyes and fair hair, cut from Tamara's own. Onkel[15] Albert comes in to inspect progress and advise but is shooed away.

'It's a secret, a surprise,' shriek the girls, spreading their arms over their creations so he cannot see.

He closes his eyes and leaves the room with pretended offence. Isa runs after him as he goes and gives him a kiss. 'Love you, Onkel.'

Vasilia's father is given a white, sheep wool beard. Also in the cast is a black cat and a fierce dog. The evil stepmother, the cook and painting the scenery take the girls another three days to complete. Albert Linke comments that life has never been so peaceful. Yet a further day is needed to write and agree the script and who should play which parts. Tamara manages this process very efficiently. Two separate, colour-coded texts are produced. Now comes the first night performance to the family. This also requires much preparation.

They get Onkel Albert's permission to pull the high backed wooden bench from by the fire, in front of the kitchen door leading to the bedrooms. He helpfully hangs a curtain over the top of the door for them and shows them how it can be tied back. The girls crouch behind the bench and the spectators sit in the kitchen. The puppets are held by their bulrush stems to show over the back of the wooden seat. The audience is quite big, made up of all of the family who ran away from the CheKa together.

The play starts:

The scene is outside Vasilia's cottage

> COMMENTATOR (Tamara, grown-up voice)

Vasilia, her father and her stepmother live together at the edge of the forest. Her evil stepmother wants to be rid of Vasilia. She wants her father's house and money. Vasilia's father has gone to the market to buy grain

> STEPMOTHER (Tamara, nasty voice)

---

[15] With two Uncle Alberts in the family, the girls use the German *Onkel* for Albert Vaatz and the Russian *Dya Dya* for Albert Linke.

Vasilia, sweet will you go to my dear sister in the forest and ask for a needle and thread to sew yourself a shirt?

                    VASILIA (Isa, sweet voice)

Of course, Mother.

                    COMMENTATOR (Tamara, grown-up voice)

But before Visalia goes into the forest, she visits her real aunt for advice. She tells her that the woman in the woods is the wicked witch Baba Yaga who eats children. She gives her a red ribbon, some oil, some ham, and two bones, and says, 'You will know what to do when the time comes.'

VASILIA struggles through a dense, dark forest constructed of fir tree twigs. She arrives at the witch's house. This enters the stage, right, walking on chicken's feet. (The girls managed to salvage real chicken feet when a cockerel was recently slaughtered.) VASILIA passes through the door. At the same time, the cardboard wall turns, and she is inside the house. Filling almost the whole wall, to the right of the door, is painted a large oven with bright flames created of foil from sweets.

                    Enter BABA YAGA, cackling wickedly

                    VASILIA (Isa, sweet voice)

Good morning aunty. My mother sent me to ask for a needle and thread to sew a shirt.

                    BABA YAGA (Isa, croaky voice)

Very well, I will go and look. While I am gone, you must finish my sewing for me.

                    COMMENTATOR (Tamara, grown-up voice)

VASILIA starts sewing but sees it is a live flower, partly stitched on

                    VASILIA (Isa, sweet voice)

Poor little flower. How are you?

					FLOWER (Tamara)

Vasilia I am imprisoned, please undo my stitches. I want to be free.

					(VASILIA does so)

					FLOWER

Your aunt is the wicked witch Baba Yaga. You must run away as quickly as you can.

					(Flower flies away)

					BABA YAGA (Isa, croaky voice, from outside)

Cook! Get water for the pot and wood for the fire and wash that sweet little girl, so she is ready to cook.

					VASILIA (Isa, sweet voice, to the cook)

Here, have my pretty red kerchief and why don't you chop less wood and carry the water in a sieve?

					COOK

Does so

Laughs happily

					BABA YAGA (Isa, croaky voice)

					(From outside)

Vasilia, are you sewing my sweet niece, are you sewing?

					VASILIA (Isa, sweet voice)

I'm sewing my aunt, I'm sewing

					COMMENTATOR (Tamara, grown-up voice)

VASILIA goes to the door to run away, but a big black cat bares its claws threatening to take out her eyes. VASILIA gives it the ham, her real aunt gave her.

					(VASILIA and CAT act the scene)

					COMMENTATOR (Tamara, grown-up voice)

	The CAT wipes his whiskers

CAT (Tamara, meow voice)

Take this napkin and comb. Put your ear to the ground and when you hear Baba Yaga getting close, throw the napkin on the ground. When she gets near again, throw down the comb. You will see what happens.

VASILIA (Isa, sweet voice)

Thank you, sweet cat.

(She gives it a kiss.)

Scene changes from house interior back to forest

COMMENTATOR (Tamara, grown-up voice)

Vasilia dashes out of the door and starts running but two fierce dogs, with sharp teeth, come chasing and growling. She throws them the bones, and they let her go.

She comes to a gate. It is thrashing to, and fro has sharp teeth and will not let Vasilia through. She oils its hinges, and the gate opens up and lets her pass. There is a nasty birch tree in her path that lashes her across her face, but she ties the red ribbon around a branch. So the birch tree bows and shows her the way

Vasilia, dogs, gate and birch tree act the scenes

Difficult scene-change back to Baba Yaga's chicken-leg house.

BABA YAGA (Isa, croaky voice)

Are you sewing nicely, my niece? Are you sewing my child?

CAT (In a very rude, cheeky voice)

I am sewing ugly old aunty, I'm sewing fast.

COMMENTATOR (Tamara, grown-up voice)

Baba Yaga comes rushing into the house. Vasilia has gone, and so has the flower. She tries to beat the cat.

BABA YAGA (Isa, croaky voice)

Why did you let her go? Why did you not tear her eyes out?

CAT

She gave me some tasty ham and was kind. You have never given me anything.

Back to the outside scene

Baba Yaga shakes the gate in anger

BABA YAGA (Isa, croaky voice)

Screams of rage

GATE

Well, you have never painted me nor put oil on my hinges. This little girl poured over a can-full, and I no longer squeak.

Baba Yaga beats the trunk of the birch tree with her stick, in frustration

TREE

You left me bare summer and winter. This little girl tied a red silk ribbon on me

Back to witch's house scene and then forest again

COMMENTATOR (Tamara, grown-up voice)

Baba Yaga rushes back to her house, jumps into her mortar and pestle and storms through the fields and meadows. Vasilia presses her ear to the ground and can hear her coming, so she throws down the blue scarf the cat has given her. It turns into a vast lake (a blue handkerchief.) The wicked witch has no choice but to drink it all up. When she has finished, she is so fat she can hardly fit into her mortar. She sets off again. After a while, Vasilia puts her ear to the ground, once more, and decides it is time to see what magic the comb will do. It turns immediately into an impenetrable forest. Baba Yaga stops. She uses her teeth and manages to chew through half the forest, but she breaks all her teeth and has to give up. This is good because in future she will not be able to eat any more children.

(Acted as the commentator talks)

Scene change. Back at home

FATHER (Tamara)

Where is my little Vasilia?

          STEPMOTHER (Tamara, nasty voice)

She is probably in the woods picking flowers. I sent her to her aunt hours ago, and she has not returned.

          FATHER (Tamara)

That's not likely. It's much too dark. I'm worried.

Just then Vasilia dashes in, breathless

          VASILIA (Isa, sweet voice)

Papa, Papa, mother sent me to my aunt to get a needle and thread, but that aunt is the wicked witch Baba Yaga and wanted to eat me.

          FATHER (Tamara)

Ach de Bozhe moi! (Oh my God!) How terrible. Where is my axe? I must kill that wicked woman.

          COMMENTATOR (Tamara, grown-up voice)

Father and daughter hug. The evil aunt runs away in fright and is never seen again. Vasilia and her father live happily together for many, many years.

    There is loud applause and clapping from the audience. First, the puppets bow together and then each appears one by one. The girls know the proper routine from their visits to the Opera house. Then the two puppet masters, themselves, creep out, stiff from crouching and flushed red with happiness and excitement. They also bow to the applause.

    Everything did not go entirely smoothly. There was a whispering behind the bench as to who should speak next and then some giggling when the wrong puppet said the wrong thing. But the performance brings back memories of warm bed-time stories to both the children and grown-ups. It is a happy relief from the worries around them.

    The Linke children beg to be allowed to produce their own show. Mary Linke organises a conference with her younger brothers to agree on what should be the subject of their play. Tamara and Isa have already decided on Rumpelstiltskin for their next production. The challenge, however, is where to find bulrushes in Odessa.

Chapter 19 – Revenge

It is early September, and the Whites have been in control of for just two weeks. Paul and family have only just arrived. Now it is possible to wear normal smart dress again and not to be frightened or ashamed to be bourgeois. Both men and women who can afford it and who had not destroyed their clothes, for fear that their discovery would label them as bourgeois, dress up with enthusiasm and parade the streets to convince themselves and others that everything is, and will be, alright. The cafés in and around Deribasovskaya somehow manage to find something to serve, even if it is ersatz coffee made of dried dandelion root. It seems to Paul that many hope that just sitting in the sun, chatting and behaving as if things are normal will make them so. In the sunny, early autumn, the Odessa streets bubble with - what Paul is convinced is - false optimism. Having just escaped from Franzfeld only thirty kilometres away and seeing how the Bolsheviks manage to manipulate the population and the force and hatred with which they punish both those who are against them and also the doubters, strengthens his determination to leave the country, and soon.

Some people are making lots of money. An unhealthy mix of fear and hedonism is in the atmosphere. *Enjoy yourself before it is too late,* seems to be the attitude of many. Both food and entertainment venues are doing well. Offerings range from street vendors selling boiled and roasted sweet corn, melon slices or ice cream, to smart restaurants doing their best to serve gourmet food but at crazy prices. In entertainment, the buskers on the street seem able to persuade passers-by to throw them coins and the theatre and opera still function. The cinema has taken hold, although its programme is minimal, and repeats itself. The less salubrious activities in the red-light district near the harbour are thriving, as is gambling. It is still warm enough to swim, and both the Langeron beach in Odessa and that at Lustdorf are busy. There is no market for cars. In any case, Paul's vehicles have all been vandalised and now, instead of the Bolsheviks, the White military requisitions any petrol supplies that are found. Property is still changing hands so lawyers and bankers are kept occupied and the administration is trying to function again. There are real policemen on the street, not thugs demanding to see your hands.

On one of these warm autumn days, Paul walks from his apartment down Marazlievskaya towards the harbour. At the bottom, on the corner where it turns left into the narrower Bariatinsky Lane, towards the centre of town, he sees a farmer's cart loaded with water-melons parked on the kerb. A soldier, with his back to him, in the dishevelled uniform of Denikin's White cavalry, is unloading melons into the greengrocers.

A soldier on short leave, earning a little on the side. Good luck to him, Paul thinks. He then notices the unusual red hair. Could it be? No, impossible! He can hardly believe his eyes. Am I fooling myself? A Red Bolshevik, an extreme and dedicated Bolshevik, dressed in the uniform of the White army? Then, as the soldier passes the melons into the shop, he catches a profile view.

Yes, it is! It is the Bolshevik who has twice tried to have me shot and was probably instrumental in having the CheKa search for me in the German villages and quite possibly also, for Carl's death. Paul checks again and convinces himself he is right.

I will have my revenge! I will make this Bolshevik suffer the same experience that I suffered: the freezing of the blood, the inner feeling of departing from this world, that of total despair.

Two White Army soldiers stand guard, within earshot, at an official building just along the street. He includes these in his plan. However, as he owes the Bolshevik his life, he will give like-for-like and not denounce him. Paul moves quietly behind and taps the Bolshevik on the shoulder, who turns in surprise.

With a stern face, he asks, precisely as the Bolshevik had done only two months before, 'Do you remember who I am?'

The Bolshevik's face goes white, and Paul can see that the redhead knows exactly who he is, and he relishes the fear that he can almost feel spreading down his victim's spine.

'No, no' He stammers.

'Then, I will tell you. I am the one who stood close to here, just like you, further up this same street, only two months ago and who you ordered to have shot by your Bolshevik thugs. Be so good as to stand against this same wall, so I can make the same request of the soldiers there to shoot you. You will not even live to see today's sunset!'

This once threatening bully slumps and seems to shrink in size.

In a shaking and offended voice, he complains, 'Then you lied to me. You said you were a foreigner, a German citizen and were not interested or involved in our Russian revolution and did not want to be mixed up in it. If that is true, you would not wish to denounce me to the militiaman. It is not fair.'

This insolent reply annoys Paul, and he answers, 'I did not say I would denounce you but that I could, and I confirm that I am a German citizen and that I want to go to Germany and leave your bloody, dirty, stupid revolution forever. What you call Red power is no longer a revolution.'

'What is it then?'

'It is a dog-eat-dog plundering of the whole people, torture, murder and death without reason and without end. How did you get hold of that uniform? A convinced Bolshevik yet in the uniform of the cavalry of Denikin's army? You must be a spy; otherwise, you would never wear that uniform. Explain yourself!'

If the Bolshevik went white when he first saw Paul, he next goes bright red, and his face returns to that of the beast Paul had seen before and in an angry but quiet voice says, 'I refuse to answer your question. You are a foreigner and are not allowed to meddle in our revolution. You said so yourself, so why do you ask me these questions?' He adds sarcastically, 'If you really want to know, then denounce me to the militiaman, but I will tell you nothing.'

Paul realises that this sly, casual reply comes because the redhead has sensed that Paul will not reveal him to the Whites. Paul now begins to wonder whether or not to do so after all. He considers the whole, military, political and moral situation a mess, a dog's breakfast.

But he answers, 'All right then, you do not have to tell me. I am just curious about your unusual uniform and will not denounce you. I am a foreigner and will keep my word. However, young man, I am sorry for you. You are wrong. Improve yourself. Give up the Reds, go over to the Whites and when they win, be part of the new, free, beautiful Russia.'

'I will stick with the Reds, I will not serve the Whites, and what I am wearing is just a masquerade. This stitched-together uniform is my insurance. I believe in my Reds. What your White generals offer is the return of the Tsar and to all the old suffering of the poor. I will not betray the Reds.'

Paul now sees him less as a traitor and more as an unfortunate, misguided young man. The Bolshevik smiles and takes Paul by the arm. He doesn't resist.

'Let's get closer to the cart and inspect the melons so that passers-by and the soldiers will assume you want to buy.'

What he had said about the White generals and the Tsar stinks of the propaganda that fills the Bolshevik papers, thinks Paul, that one cannot trust the White generals as they seek the return of an unlimited autocratic monarchy. He is a young man and has clearly been brainwashed by this propaganda.

So Paul asks, 'Have you not noticed how Jews hold most of the senior positions in the Revolution? Trotsky, Bronstein, Sinoweff, Apfelbaum, Teklow, Nachamkes, Kamenew, Rosenfeld, Radek, Sobelsohn? The Jews lead the people's tribunals. I have seen it in Odessa. The Jews and Jewesses are also prominent in the CheKa. Have you not heard of the 'beautiful Rosa?' How the Whites are taken to the Zhdanov building in Ekaterininskaya Place, imprisoned and then murdered with a shot in the neck? Will you still not believe me that the Jews lead this bloody revolution?

'And what about Lenin, Bucharin and the other Russians?'

'Those are just a few. Think, do you really want to help the Bolsheviks drag poor Mother Russia to Hell?'

'I will think about it.'

'Good and I will repay what you did for me. I will not expose you. We are now even. You are free. But do not serve the Bolsheviks!'

In a final gesture, Paul buys a watermelon and, as he walks away, hoists it high in one hand, in a farewell salute to the Red-head. The Bolshevik gives a loose-handed, mock military salute in return.

Paul has an interesting story to tell to Sophia when he arrives home. He is elated. He has got his revenge, and there is at least a chance that the Bolshevik will convert to the Whites. However, on the day before the family's eventual departure from Odessa, fate catches up with the Bolshevik. He apparently makes the wrong decision.

Chapter 20 – Café Franconi

The lift is not working. No electricity again. So Paul takes the steps to get to his apartment. He wants to check how the electricians and the painters are getting on with the refurbishment. Halfway up the last flight, he hears,

'Pavel, Pavel Fredrikovich! Stop! Is that you?'

He turns and sees Alexander, a co-fugitive in their Bolshevik-in-Alexander Park confrontation. He backs down three steps to face his old friend coming up. They embrace and exchange three Russian kisses to the left and right. Paul ponders, when he gets to Germany, will it be more of a stiff, formal handshake? And hopes it will not also be a heal-click - a custom he noticed some of the German officers, when in Odessa, still followed.

They are standing uncomfortably on two steps, so Paul pulls his friend up to his landing. Still holding, arms stretched, they look each other in the eyes. Together both ask ' How are you' and 'How have you survived' and then both try to respond at the same time.

Paul laughs. 'Let's have a coffee together tomorrow.' And then with concern in his voice, 'Is Vadim still with us?'

'Yes, he like me went and stayed with his servants in the Peresypce (A poorer area of town) quarter. They looked after us and said when it was safe to go and walk in the street. Now we protect our servants, against any who say they are Bolshevik sympathisers. It is a terrible mixed-up world. How about tomorrow, Café Robina in Ekaterininskaya or the Franconi, opposite?' Alexandr continues.

'Let's savour Little Paris and do the Franconi,'

Agreed, I'll go next door and tell Vadim. Tomorrow morning at eleven then.'

Paul is relieved and happy. Two of his closest Russian friends are still alive. Back in the apartment, where Sophia is supervising the measuring for new curtains, he tells her the good news. Now their flat is again looking something like before, it is very tempting for him to change his mind and to stay after all. But his frightening experiences with the Bolsheviks and the news that they are steadily advancing, firms his resolve to leave with the family. But the challenge remains, how?

Next morning Paul is first at the Franconi. He has dressed for the occasion, all in black with a burgundy waistcoat, sporting gold watch chain; a stand-up collar with a matching burgundy cravat. He hands his top hat to the waiter and selects a table on the first-floor balcony from where he can watch the crowd. The waiter, formal in black with a long white apron, seems a little put out when Paul says he will wait for his friends to arrive before ordering. The crowd below looks content enough, and among it he sees his two friends approaching. They too are 'properly' dressed. Today is something of a celebration, a reunion. As Alexander and Vadim get close, they wave up at him.

The two join the table and congratulate Paul on his choice of seating. There is a genuinely warm Russian greeting all round. Vadim hands the waiter the red-silk-lined cloak that he sports, in spite of the warm early September sun. Alexei, offers his trademark silver-topped stick, which Paul is convinced, holds a little vodka in its handle.

They order coffee and Paul suggests ice cream, for which the Franconi is famous, and both accede. They relive together the Alexander Park incident and agree how lucky they had been to escape. They could all have been shot, only for Odessa to be freed minutes later. Paul is about to recount his recent experience with the Bolshevik and the water-melons but stops himself. He decides that his friends might find it difficult to understand and accept his reason for allowing such a dangerous revolutionary to go free.

The ice creams are savoured, and the different flavours exchanged and compared. The dishes are cleared, and they have sufficient coffee to keep them supplied for a while. Vadim and Alexander are curious to know Paul's story of survival but are even more anxious to tell him of their role in the re-occupation of Odessa by Denikin's AFSR (Armed Forces of Southern Russia) on the 23 August. This suits Paul for at present he is not at all keen to relive the experiences of recent weeks. Vadim pulls a folded paper from an inside pocket. It is a marked-up map of Odessa that he carefully flattens out between the coffee cups.

He starts. 'We could tell the Reds were not in a strong position, with the harbour blocked by the AFSR *Cruiser Ochakov* and the British Royal Navy cruiser *HMS Caradoc.* Also, Denikin had advanced from the Crimea to Nikolayev, only sixty km to the north-east. We got the sad news of the war of the villagers with White Army support against the Reds being lost. The good thing about that battle for us in Odessa was that Red troops were taken out of the town to fight it.

'I fought in that war.' Paul can't stop himself interjecting, 'and then we had to run west to Franzfeld.'

'We know, and you must tell us all about it.' Alexander says, but continues, 'A Col. Sablin asked for volunteers to establish White armed cells in the city to support the White liberation forces when they arrived. Vadim and I volunteered for the Marazlievskaya cell and were each given a rifle. There were a dozen of us in our cell, all from Marazlievskaya, Kanatnaya or the streets in between. We had secret lessons, in cellars at night, on how to use them. The instruction was a little farcical, as we didn't fire a single shot. This was both to save ammunition and so as not to be discovered. A significant achievement of Sablin's was to 'turn' Sheykovsky, the Red commander of Bolshevik Black Sea Fleet in Odessa. He was persuaded to support the volunteers. This meant that when the Whites landed, the coastal batteries did not fire on them. '

Vadim picked up the story. 'But before that, we got terrible news. The Reds discovered Sablin's plans. He and his three lieutenants were arrested. Many cells were exposed, and the patriots ruthlessly murdered. About half the units, including ours, thank God, remained undiscovered. We don't know how or why. Anyhow,

Denikin's invasion went ahead as planned without immediate support from us. It was a surprise landing from the south, rather than the north, on the morning of the 23 August, at Chornomorsk, 25km away. They faced no initial resistance.

'Then came the good news.' This from Alexander. 'We learned that the three Red commanders in the city had fled, as soon as they learned of the attack. This left their troops leaderless. In the early afternoon a body of Red Guards, armed with howitzers, grouped at the Artillery school above the harbour. The cruisers were informed, shelled the position and the unit disintegrated in panic. There must have been communication between the ships in the harbour, Denikin and our units in Odessa. How this was achieved we do not know. Later in the afternoon, another group of Reds assembled above the Arcadia bastion, ready to defend the city against Denikin's troops. Again the cruiser captains were passed the information, and there was a similar satisfactory result.'

'This is when we played our part.' Came in Vadim. 'Three cannon shots were fired from the Arcadia battery. It was the agreed signal for the cells to come into the open and attack the Reds. But there were no Reds in sight for us to attack, so we decided to 'liberate' our apartments at Marazlievskaya 14b, still with its sign *Red Army Number 1*, hung between the balconies. We marched into the building, brandishing our weapons. First we went to the balconies and cut down the Red Army banner. It seemed that no one remained in the block, which was in a terrible mess. Not just untidy but vandalised with threatening slogans daubed in red all over the walls.

Eventually, we discovered a about twenty Reds cowering in a room. Three of them were women. All jumped up and raised their hands when we entered. They were frightened and confused and asked us what they should do. We had no idea. They appeared to be office workers rather than soldiers. But in case they could be of value to the White authorities, we ushered them down into the cellars and locked them into two store-rooms.

When we emerged back into the street, a Red rabble was streaming past our door. The Whites were chasing them from the harbour, along our Marazlievskaya and the parallel Kanatnaya, towards the railway station. We pointed our guns and demanded they surrendered. Most did, although some ran off into the park. We didn't bother to chase them. Again we were uncertain what to do and made our captives lie face-down on the pavement, and posted a guard with a rifle to make sure they remained. We must have had fifty or sixty men on that pavement by the time a White Army sergeant came and took them off our hands. We remembered to tell him about our prisoners in the cellar.'

Paul smiles internally at the image of his short, round lawyer friend, with his red-lined cloak slung around his shoulders, and a somewhat timid Alexander not quite sure what to do with his silver-topped stick, both waving their guns at hardened soldiers, and demanding they surrender.

He admits they succeeded and says, 'Well, that's the sort of war I would have liked to fight. You managed it very efficiently without firing a single shot.' This sounds a little cynical and patronising, he knows, but it is true, he would far rather not have had to fire a single shot.

There is an argument over who is to pay, which Paul wins and they then return together to Marazlievskaya. Paul collects Sophia, who is now organising the rearrangement of the furniture. She finishes her task and they walk arm in arm to Mathilde and Albert's apartment in Peter the Great Street, to be greeted by two cheerful girls. Two blocks away, they have found a family with a boy and a girl of about their age, who still have all their toys. They have played with them all day. Although their new friends are also ethnic Germans, they speak only Russian together. It is very much their first language.

Chapter 21 – Too long in Odessa

Paul's rise in spirits, following the reunion with his two old friends, plunges again two days later when he receives a surprise visitor. He recognises him immediately as Danya, one of brother Carl's longest-serving men. He looks pale and drawn.

'How are you managing?' Paul asks.

'I'm surviving, sir. Thank you. I thought you would wish to know how and why your brother came to be shot. But I must warn you it is not pleasant.'

'I appreciate your concern, but I do need to understand how it ended.'

Paul notices Isa, kneeling in front of an armchair on the other side of the room, with her doll seated in front of her on a cushion. She is patiently teaching it to read.

'Isichka darling could you go and play in the next room with Tamara, I'm sorry we need that chair.'

Once Isa had gone Danya asks, 'You know when he died?'

'Yes, the seventeenth of July according to that terrible rag, 'The Fight.' Please go on.'

***

There was a loud banging on the front door. I opened it cautiously, but was pushed aside, and a pistol waved in my face. There were four. Two dressed all in black leather. One was the commissar, another his sidekick and two young lads, in ill-matching, salvaged army uniforms and with red armbands. They smelled of alcohol. A fifth followed behind. I recognised him straight away as the man who had asked Mr Carl for some work, the previous week, saying he needed to buy food for his children. He had been given some repairs to do in the house. He avoided my look and stared purposefully ahead. He was clearly the informer.

The commissar demanded, 'Where is he?'

'Who?" I asked.'

'Capitalist Carl Vaatz, that's who. And you don't need to say. We already know.'

He pulled the informer from the back of the party and pushed him forward, in the small of his back, with the knuckles of a fist that still held his revolver.

'Come on, show us! You lot come too.' And he crooked his fingers at me and Mr Carl's two other members of staff, both women, one quite young.'

Three of us and five of them were squeezed in that claustrophobic cellar store-room. The informer pointed sheepishly at a set of shelves that appeared to be fixed permanently to the wall.

'Don't stand there, open up.' The traitor went to the shelves. He was clearly trying to find a way into a secret hiding place. The two young men watched. One rolled a cigarette and while doing so, dug his accomplice in the ribs with his elbow. 'Weren't they having a great time?' was his attitude. There was a click as the informer undid a catch at the back, and the shelves swung out into the cellar so that we had to move out of the way. There sat Mr Carl, in a space no bigger than a toilet. He must have been reading by the light of the single bulb that hung over his head. He put his book down on the box beside him and looked at us.

The commissar waved his hand, and the two young men jumped forward, each grabbed an arm and dragged Mr Carl out. He would have come out himself, given just a little time.

'Citizen Vaatz do you confess to being a capitalist, a blood-sucker and a counter-revolutionary?"

'I am Carl Vaatz and am a businessman and farmer.'

I started to leave and wanted to take the women with me because I could tell something terrible was going to happen.

'You lot stay and learn, or I must assume you are sympathisers and shoot you too.' And then to Carl, 'You have just confessed to being a blood-sucking capitalist and land-owner. In the name of the People and the Glorious Revolution, you are sentenced to death.'

'Hold him tight.' This to the two young men, who each yanked at an arm.

I couldn't comprehend what had entered these young men's souls. One still had a lit cigarette hanging from the corner of his mouth; they were boorish and grinned evilly at each other, as they leant back stretching Mr Carl out like a cross. I know it's blasphemy sir but I found myself comparing Mr Carl's situation with that of Christ on the cross.

The commissar moved behind Mr Carl, who closed his eyes and mumbled some words, but not in fear, more like a prayer and perhaps remembering his wife. The sound of the shot, in that confined space, was awful. Even the perpetrators jumped. The two women hugged close, the younger letting out a short muffled moan.

'All right, let him go. He won't run away.'

Mr Carl's body crumpled onto the stone floor. The two women looked at the commissar to confirm they were allowed and went to straighten and tidy the body. The older one closed his eyes. The younger one rescued Mr Carl's spectacles from the floor and slipped them into his top pocket. The commissar holstered his pistol, took a notebook from an upper pocket, checked his watch and made some notes.

'Official notice of this execution will appear in tomorrow's The Fight.' He proclaimed, as if to a large audience and as if that justified his action.

He said something to his lieutenant and impatiently waved his fingers at the pouch the man had on his belt. The number-two withdrew a small receipt book, adjusted the carbon paper, completed a form and handed it to his boss. While the commissar was signing, his second-in-command fished out an inkpad and stamp from the pouch on the other side of his belt. He opened the pad and presented it up, in two hands, for the commissar to place a stamp beside his signature.

With a flick of the elbow, the commissar tore off the top sheet and handed it to the informer. 'Take that to headquarters and collect your reward. Well done.'

The man grabbed the paper and hurried up the cellar stairs, avoiding our eyes. The commissar took a final satisfied look at Mr Carl's body, at us and around the cellar and also left. He was followed by the two young, louts, still behaving stupidly, grinning both at each other, and at us. Mr Carl was brave, but it was so pointless and so unfair. We show more pity when slaughtering a chicken or a pig on the farm than these heathens did in murdering Mr Carl.

Thank God that Mrs Vaatz was out, but I had to stay and inform her what had happened. It was not easy, Sir. She came back quite cheerful that the ladies group she had been helping had succeeded in finding food for some of those who were suffering most from the shortages. And there at the front door I had to tell her because Mr Carl's body was still lying in the cellar.

Danya, chokes and can say no more. Paul, who is still sitting, looking down with his head in his hands, glances up and then gets up. He stoops to put an arm round Danya's shoulders.

'Danya, brave man, I can never thank you enough for your loyalty and kindness. I know you also invited Mrs Julia to hide in your house to escape being harassed again by the CheKa. That was a real risk for you.'

Paul decides it is still better to know what happened. A small mercy, for these times, is that Carl had had a quick death and had not first been tortured. Before leaving, Danya explains where Carl is buried and reassures Paul that it had been possible to arrange for a proper Christian funeral. As Danya departs both tell each other to be careful. Alone again, Paul decides he cannot share this account with Sophia. He is not even sure whether he should pass the details on to Albert. As the two oldest brothers of the family, Albert and Carl had been very close.

***

Isa tells

I was walking home from school when two men, dressed in black-leather, started following me. I walked faster, and I could hear their big boots still coming. Although their steps did not get any quicker, the men kept getting closer. I ran into a house door and up the stairs. These went up a square atrium, and there were four landings. I got trapped on the top floor with the men facing me from the bottom of the final flight of stairs. One started to come up, so I picked up a mahogany chair from beside the wall and threw it at him. He tried to dodge, but it hit him on the leg, and he tumbled down the few steps he had come up. He jumped about on one leg, cursing and then drew his pistol at me.

I shouted, 'Go on, go on shoot. If I am dead, I'm no use to you.'

Next, I lifted up a big blue and white vase from the side-table and threatened to throw it at the next man trying to come up. They hesitated. I threw it at them anyway and dashed into the first door I could find. Slammed it shut, locked it and pushed an armchair in front; then looked around. How to escape? It was an attic room with a sloping ceiling. It had a skylight and on the low outside wall was a small door that I assumed would lead to a storage space under the eaves. I pushed open the skylight so the men would think I'd escaped onto the roof. Then I bent low and crept, through the little door, into the space under the eaves. I pulled the door closed, behind me.

I realised I was not in a cupboard but under the roof itself. This seemed to stretch right down to ground level and I could see a strip of daylight at the bottom. The roof, in fact, covered the windows of the floors below. It didn't make sense. The space between the roof and the wall was not much wider than me. Crawling on my tummy, I gradually eased myself downwards and only just managed to squeeze out through the space between the gutter and the ground. I sat up and found myself on the edge of a road, a promenade beside the sea. The sun was shining. People were walking around, quite happily, and I sat up on the ground to watch them.

I awoke, in the dark, sitting up in bed; then crept across to Tamara's. She gave me a hug and grumbled I had woken her up with my shouting.

In the morning she told me of a nasty little dream she had had two nights before. It was in an old Russian she could hardly understand, just as we had heard in the Orthodox cathedral.

An ambassador to a Tsar of long ago was returning to his country, possibly Germany, for instructions. He wrote to the Tsar complaining of the treatment he had received at a border inn. The food was poor, the bed linen dirty with bed-bugs, and the innkeeper rude and complaining about foreigners.

The Tsar's secretary sent a messenger back to the Ambassador saying, The innkeeper was summoned to St Petersburg to explain himself. His majesty was pleased to accept the man's apologies and granted his forgiveness. The innkeeper was given a good breakfast; such as he should have provided for your excellency, and then hanged.'

Tamara said she was crying when she woke up. We agreed not to tell Mama of our dreams. It would only give her more to worry about.

***

It is the end of September, and brother-in-law Albert decides that he, Cornelia and the children should get back to their estate in Cherson, near the Crimea. Denikin's troops also have control there, and he can better assess the situation, pack things and get ready to leave if circumstances again deteriorate, as Paul is predicting they will.

Soon after, in the first week of October, Paul and Sophia are ready to put their restored property up for sale with all its fittings and furnishings. It is a good time because General Denikin is in town and confidence is growing. Paul is surprised at the interest shown by those who have escaped from the Bolshevik occupied parts of the country. The best offer comes from a Count Vlad, who Paul assumes is a Baltic Russian from his name. He had arrived with his family and two large carts of possessions. How he had managed to get these through the war-ravaged Ukrainian countryside is a mystery. He still seems to have faith in the White army, and they conclude a deal within two days. The means of payment presents a challenge as the rouble has crashed in value and the kerenk, introduced by the short-lived Kerensky government, has almost no value. So the settlement is made in a mix of jewellery, gold and silver coins, war bonds and Tsarist -or Romanov -roubles. Paul is relieved to have received anything and to be rid of what he considers to be an encumbrance.

The coming October and November are terrible months for Paul. No news on how to get out of Odessa and to Germany. The self-defence unit that the Society of Black Sea Colonists has created is having only limited success in defending the small village farmers from roaming robber bands, let alone the ever more professional, requisitioning Red Army units. But in Odessa itself most still appear to be happy and confident. He can't comprehend their blindness.

He is frustrated. His best books, those he hadn't left behind in the flat, are packed; ready to be shipped when an opportunity arises. He finds it difficult to find something constructive to do. Earlier attempts had shown he couldn't even teach his daughters without getting angry and making them cry.

Early one morning, he walks alone, through the still damp grass, to a remote corner of Alexander Park. There, sheltered by thick bushes, he starts to yell and shout and curse. He spits out the most extreme profanities he can drag from his memory. Paul curses the whole shitty situation. Again he blames everyone and anyone, the Bolsheviks and all the many self-serving factions participating in the revolution, the provisional governments, the separatists such as Poles, Ukrainians and Romanians; then the Tsar, the Allies, French, English and Greek and the German-Austrian Alliance, the gods in general and God himself. Why, why are they all so ignorant and stupid? Why so cruel? Why this awful, terrible hell? Why, especially poor Carl, who had never harmed anybody? He drums with the side of his fists against the smooth grey bark of the large beech tree that he stands beneath. He holds the trunk between his hands and bangs his head against it, slowly and softly in despair. And then just stands, head leaning against the tree breathing regularly. He straightens, takes a few deep breaths, wipes his eyes and mouth, first with the back of his hand and then with a clean white handkerchief pulled from his inside pocket. He folds it carefully and returns it to his pocket. He pushes back his shoulders and walks determinedly back to his brother's Odessa house. He and his family must survive and will survive!

He compares the two months they have now been stuck in Odessa with the short two weeks they had spent in Franzfeld. There they had always been nervous, on tenterhooks, waiting to be exposed, worried that something nasty would happen, and it did, often. It seems there was a threat on their lives almost every other day. Here in Odessa, they are safe, but for how long?

The air of optimism is unreal with the bulk of the population appearing to assume that the Whites can still win. They apparently do not believe or choose to ignore the growing strength of the Bolshevik forces. This frustrates and depresses him, and he is getting more and more impatient waiting for the opportunity to leave and emigrate to Germany. He is convinced that the Reds will soon again achieve the upper hand and retake Odessa. He considers Denikin's White army has become far too weak. The Allied forces are entirely disinterested and ineffective. French and Greek troops had arrived in August, with their small tanks, shortly before the family returned to Odessa from Franzfeld. But they are useless, sit around and do not bother themselves with the revolution. Instead, they spend their time offering passers-by Cognac for sale. Often the bottles contain nothing more than tea. Paul takes a chance and is lucky that his purchase is genuine. So they have a little toast in the evening that an early means of escape will somehow appear.

Mid morning a couple of days later Paul and Vadim walk through Ekaterininskaya Square and are surprised to see a large group of English sailors gathered outside the Zhdanov building. It has become the unofficial museum of Bolshevik barbarism. Visitors are shown round the cells and told of the perverse and extreme tortures that the Cheka had inflicted on their victims. The liberated population of the town, foreign representatives and the armed forces supporting the Whites all visit the museum.

Paul summons his courage and tests his English on one of the naval officers standing a little apart from his men.

'How do you like Odessa?'

The officer raises his eyebrows in surprise and smiles. Paul hopes this because of his fantastic English but may be it's just being asked the question by a stranger.

He responds, 'Very much. You have a beautiful city. A great shame it has been so damaged.'

On the spur, Paul invites him and a fellow officer for a coffee and a chat. They accept willingly. They are as interested to learn about Odessa and the Revolution, as Paul and Vadim are to hear what is the Allied strategy. The hosts guide their guests to a little place, a short way up Ekaterininskaya. On the way Paul points out his shattered Mercedes show room at the corner of the square. He has made no attempt to restore it. It is a total loss. His new English friends are sympathetic.

'Good God. What are you going to do? Will you get compensation?'

Paul smiles wryly,' I doubt it and what can I sell? The Germans are now our enemies.'

Vadim doesn't say anything but gives Paul a knowing look and a little smile. It's best these Englishmen think they are talking to two Russians. Paul can't decide whether the British are friends or enemies. If I am a White Russian they are my friends, as a German, my enemies. But I am both.

Once the coffees arrive Paul starts with the important question, 'What is the Allied strategy? Will the British continue to give their support?'

The senior of the two; he has more gold rings on his sleeve, replies. 'I wish I knew. The politicians can't make up their minds, which makes it impossible for us here at the front. But I am fairly sure we will be here for some time, yet. And you, what are your plans?'

Vadim answers, 'Some have already run away to safety, many still hope to, but the ways of getting out are limited. By sea there is hardly any transport and by land one would have to pass through Red territory. So unless you are very rich and can bribe, you are stuck and just have to hope that the Allies will continue to support General Denikin and his army.'

'Many, however, are optimistic and some are making a lot of money buying and selling. I have to admit I am not one of them and will get out as soon as I can.' Says Paul.

'Where would you go?'

'I am not sure, somewhere in Europe, perhaps France. I can speak the language.'

Again that knowing look from Vadim.

'You speak French as well. How many languages can you speak?

'Four if you accept English as one.'

'You certainly can. That's impressive. All I know is a bit of school Latin.'

Paul could admit to that too, and is glad he is not asked for his fourth language. He decides it is best not to show off. But he does mention that he had visited London in 1902 when he was still a student, and that sets the discussion off in another direction.

They sit chatting a while longer and then walk with their new English friends to the Grand Opera. It like most buildings has gunshot holes in its walls and many windows are broken but it nevertheless impresses, especially when they venture inside and stare up at the white and gold stairway with its gilded statues. They go along Deribasovskaya, show their visitors the cathedral and then back again past Catherine the Great's statue to the top of the

Potemkin steps. All around their little circuit there is a depressing mix of former grandeur with recent random destruction.

The officers thank Paul and Vadim for their coffee and the tour. Both pairs wish each other well. The officers turn and wave back again when almost half way down the steps.

Bolshevist House of Torture, 1919. British sailors visiting the CheKa torture chambers in Ekaterininskaya Square. [The Times, December 1919]

Only a few days after their meeting with the naval officers the remaining Greek troops leave. The French stay longer, in fact to a time after the family manages to escape Odessa, but they only bring bad luck to the city. It would have been better had they never arrived. Because of the French presence in Odessa, the White army gains confidence and advances in the north but then, when the French suddenly depart by sea, the Odessa end of the White front is blown wide open, and the Reds quickly retake the town together with many Whites and all their wealthy possessions. The rumour is that the French General D'Anselm accepted a several million Roubles bribe in gold, from the Reds, to leave. The official reason given for the departure is the outbreak of revolutions in France, led by extreme socialists and even communists.

Chapter 22 – The steamship Arta

Perhaps that toast in Cognac, a few days before, worked because the fantastic news arrives that the German steam freighter, *Arta*, has docked in the harbour. It will be leaving for Hamburg in just two days, on the 6th December[16], according to the calendar now used by most of the civilised world and introduced to Russia by the Bolsheviks. This, in Paul's view, being the only good decision they ever made. The ship will transport any remaining Germans free of charge back to Germany. It is to be the last such ship to sail! The family rushes to pack everything.

Paul organises the non-trivial task of transferring and loading four large wooden crates on to the freighter. These contain, as Paul has ensured, many books including the complete works of the Russian classics such as Tolstoy, Pushkin, Dostoyevsky, but also Shakespeare and Byron in Russian and Mark Twain in German. Most are illustrated and with gold edging. Not only Paul's and Sophia's but also those of the children. Paul remembers packing the tattered Pinocchio that he had also had read to him as a child. He includes the large samovar that has been the centre-piece of the dining room since before his time. So, although they lose most of their toys, the girls' books will accompany them. Then there are the two small but relatively heavy boxes of valuables, mostly silver and jewellery that are kept close by, one with Sophia and one with Paul. Paul smiles when he recalls how they had managed to smuggle these past the Red guards, and how the children had played their part in the subterfuge.

---

[16] New calendar

A late addition is a packet of smoked meat and sausages, a present from brother Albert. Two weeks before he had returned to his Karlovka estate, in a friendly White Army officer's car, to check how things were. On arrival he found everything in ruin, ransacked and destroyed. The few old employees that remained were polite but totally disillusioned and confused by events, some even begging him to return. There was very little for him to salvage, nothing of value and only a few items of sentimental value. He had collected a few photographs and books and at the back of his old cellar storeroom managed to rescue some hidden preserved meats. For Paul, Albert's present, as well as providing a welcome addition to the limited diet available on board, would, during their sea journey, be exchanged for favours such as a better sleeping bunk or alternative food.

The girls had packed their Baba Yaga puppets lovingly in a cardboard box after their successful show. Now Mama is suggesting they should be left behind. There is too much to take, and they can always make new ones. Both Isa and Tamara beg and beg, and Sophia is close to giving in when Tamara unties the strings and opens the lid. As she does so, a cloud rises out of the box and floats to the ceiling — all gasp.

Tamara shouts, 'Mama look!'

The puppets disintegrate as they watch. The box is mostly full of fluff. Isa puts her hand in to inspect her Vasilia more closely, and another cloud blows into the room. Sophia realises that the bulrushes have seeded and formed fluffy pappii. Tamara takes out Baba Yaga, still more pappii rise to the ceiling to be blown around the kitchen by the breeze from the open window. The girls go to inspect further, but it is getting chaotic, and before they can do so, Sophia grabs the lid and slaps it firmly on the box. Even this creates another cloud. Seeds are floating everywhere, and all are waving their hands in front of their faces and holding their breath. Sophia is trying to work out how she can get rid of these floaters.

'Take your box outside. There you can inspect to your heart's content.'

She passes the box to back to Tamara, one had below and one, holding down the lid, Isa follows her sister into the garden. They open the lid slowly. In spite of their care, another cloud of seeds on their tiny parachutes floats out. They lay the puppets side-by-side on the rough grass at the edge of the courtyard. Vasilia still has a face. This is because of the white flour paste they had used. She also has her hair; Tamara's hair. Otherwise, she is all loose fluff or naked stick. The witch has her nose and not much else. The Father has his beard. The rest of the cast are all wrecks. Just the cat and the dogs, made from sheep's wool, are intact, as is the gate. The scenery is also unharmed. They decide to keep these as souvenirs and, perhaps, for presenting a repeat performance in Germany. Mama will not object. They hide the puppet remains in the grass and weeds. When they return to the kitchen, poor Mama is still chasing the floating seeds around the kitchen with a wet tablecloth.

*****

The family spends the final day waiting to board the *Arta* with Albert and Mathilde. Oma, Sophia's mother, had already said her goodbyes in Grossliebental, but that does not relieve her sorrow. At the last hour, Aunt Julia, now a widow, also decides to join them. Sophia is happy to have female company, and Paul agrees that it is a sensible thing to do. The families sit together in the evening over Russian lemon tea and in front of a decent fire that they are lucky to have. The girls play quietly together; with the doll they are each allowed to take with them on the journey. The adults reminisce and start their long goodbyes, Paul arguing the others should come with him and they still persuading him to stay. The girls eavesdrop and try to make sense of the conversation.

As they are talking the maid comes in and says there is a young lady in the kitchen crying and urgently wanting to speak to Mr Paul Vaatz. He finds a Russian peasant girl, simply dressed with a covered head, seated on the chair beside the kitchen fire. Paul pulls a chair to sit opposite her. She wipes away tears with the corner of her shawl and explains that her husband has been arrested and is waiting to be tried by the military tribunal, to be shot as a Bolshevik. Paul is the only one who can save him, and she begs him to go to the court and swear that her husband is not a Bolshevik but a White. Further, her husband is suspicious that Paul has denounced him to the Whites.

She can only be talking about the Bolshevik. Paul never learned his name.

Her story makes Paul realise just how efficiently the Red spy system has been working. They knew where he and family had been living with Mrs Van Dych in the outskirts and later in Grossliebenthal and the other German villages. They also know that, after selling his Odessa property, he has now moved in with his in-laws.

However, he stresses to the girl that he has kept his promise and has not exposed her husband. Someone else must have done so. He explains that even if he wants to help it is not possible to do so because the military offices are now closed and he is leaving very early the next morning on the last ship. He adds that they are even. Her husband had saved Paul from being shot, and he has returned that favour. She leaves, and that is the end of Paul's episode with the Bolshevik.

He is not surprised that the Bolshevik has been discovered for, as they had experienced in Alexander Park, he did not hide his strong communist views. It could also have been that Vadim, Paul's lawyer friend, had finally tracked him down and exposed him to the authorities. Paul feels genuinely sorry for the girl and has a slight feeling of guilt that he has not offered to help. She seems innocent, and he realises that had it been one of his own, who had been in danger, he would somehow have managed to make contact with the head of the military court, even though the offices were closed. The head of the court could easily be a major who Paul knew socially and, if not, would almost certainly be a White officer who knew one of Paul's several senior military friends, stationed in Odessa. Unlike for the young wife, however, he has no sympathy for the Bolshevik. He thinks it more than likely that, with his evident knowledge of the Vaatz family, he was instrumental both in arranging for the murder of his dear brother and for the CheKa being guided where to look for his family in the German villages. Paul never learns what happens but has to admit to himself it is probable that the military court sentenced the Bolshevik to death.

The family departs for the harbour just after five o'clock the following morning, on the 6th December[17]. It is still dark. Albert and

Mathilde come on board, as do three cousins. When these see the rough conditions the family will have to endure, they try again to persuade them to change their minds, as they are confident that the Whites will win. Paul is not even close to agreeing. The experiences that he has suffered during the last year convince him that his family and he will be far safer and happier in Germany. However, he reassures his relatives by promising to return if conditions improve.

So after hugs, tears and kisses, on a cold, dull morning, Paul, Sophia, Tamara and Isa, together with Aunt Julia, are waving goodbye from the ship's rail. They sail out into the Black Sea. Today it is truly black; black in colour and black in mood. Paul grips the railing tightly and stares. The harbour quays are already out of sight. The east-facing buildings on the bluff above the Potemkin Steps shine palely through the light morning mist, as the wintery sun appears over the horizon. He can see the reflection from the white stone of the buildings where their apartment is located, high up above the harbour, although all are now too small to separate one block from another.

He sighs loudly and gives silent thanks to God that he can take his family out of danger from this disintegrating country. The feeling of fear and claustrophobia he has been living with is evaporating. In Odessa it was that of being hemmed-in by enemies and wondering when they would break in, and they did more than once. And when they did, the claustrophobia got worse. The enemy was everywhere. One had to pretend to be one of them, or die. He shuddered when he recalled that in Ekaterininskaya Square he and Sophia had had to cheer when the shout went up to seek out and liquidate the entire bourgeoisie of the city. The same sensitive play-acting was needed in Franzfeld to stay alive. No more. They can all relax.

His relief is mixed with a great sadness and concern for the loved ones they are leaving behind. Paul doubts whether they will we ever see family or homeland again. He finds it impossible to comprehend that both Alberts have decided to stay behind; eldest brother, together with him, having had a brother butchered by the Cheka, and brother-in-law having been in their clutches, forced to watch executions and hearing the cries of those being tortured. He

---

[17] By the new, Gregorian calendar

feels anger too, for all the wealth and property that has been taken from them – an unfair reward for the generations that had worked so hard to improve the land and to bring prosperity to their beloved Odessa. Paul hurts inside for brother Carl who had been so happy on his estate. He really should be standing here on the rail beside them with Julia. He so easily could have been.

Sophia thinks of her mother Oma, and cries – no she howls, but within herself, and without tears, so not to upset the children. Like Paul, she also worries about her older sister, Mathilde and Albert. Why had they not taken this last opportunity to get out? And brother-in-law Albert and Paul's sister Nellie, at their estate in Cherson close to the Crimea, have they been able to leave? She hopes they are being sensible. Lives are far more important than property. Julia also cries, 'Carl. Carl, Carlushka, where are you? I want you, I need you.' But, like Sophia's it is a silent cry. She puts her left hand on Isa's head and strokes it. Isa looks up, stretches out her arm and hugs her aunt close.

Carl and Oma at his Schastlivka Estate

The five remain standing together in the cold until Odessa disappears behind the mauve, misty headland of the banks of the

Dniester estuary with the Turkish fort of Ackermann at its point. Sophia finds it unreal to think, that not so long ago she had viewed Ackerman from the cemetery hill in Grossliebental, together with the girls. Paul places a hand lovingly over Sophia's on the rail. She pauses, looks at him and puts her other hand on his. Another pause and he puts his free hand on hers. She then quickly pulls her hand out from under and places it on top. It becomes a game that ends in a flurry and a hug and a kiss. The girls eye this childish nonsense with superior surprise.

As they both put their hands back on the rail, Paul wonders why Sophia's hand had felt so different, unfamiliar. Ah, he remembers, it was because she had removed all her rings following Mathilda's awful experience at the CheKa. Now, Paul smiles, she must wear them again. During their flight, she had had to sacrifice some jewellery, but she had managed to save her most treasured rings.

The girls get impatient. Isa pulls at Sophia's hand and Tamara at Paul's coat. They want to go below deck to explore where they will eat and sleep. They are excited by the novelty of this new adventure. Aunt Julia joins in the exploration.

Paul's family, although not sleeping on soft couches and in luxury but on wooden soldier's benches, are soon happy to be steaming peacefully half-way around Europe to Germany. The bulk of the passengers are ex-prisoners of war. They are as pleased as Paul and family to be going home and keep everyone cheerful with their mouth organ playing and the singing of traditional songs. They also like to spoil Tamara and Isa with their attention, many of them no doubt thinking of their own children at home. When the sea is not too rough, the two girls explore all over the ship and make friends with both crew and other passengers. As they are the only youngsters on board, everyone takes an interest in them, and they are somewhat spoilt. The cook gives them a treat from time to time, such as an apple or something sweet and they realise how lucky they are as the standard food is basic and boring – dried beans or lentils in which they find small worms. The novelty of corned beef is a little more acceptable, but they soon have enough of that too.

Paul, Sophia and Julia are happy to play their part on board, to collect in groups to peel potatoes and to share other chores. Sophia manages to charm the captain, and he shows her and Paul the bridge and its controls and occasionally invites them to his cabin for a drink. In return, Paul can present him with a farm-made sausage or two. The family is separated for sleeping, Paul with the soldiers and Sophia, Julia and the girls with the seven only other ladies on board. Nevertheless, the wooden bunks and hammocks are cosy enough and comfortable, as they have brought their own warm bedding with them. The girls share a wooden bed hung on four chains. This is designed to cancel the movement of the swaying ship. In practice, it seems to enhance the swing. However, as they appear to be immune to seasickness, they enjoy the excitement of the rough sea.

The Allies allow no one to disembark at any of the ports on the way. All through the journey, either English or French warships escort the *Arta*, and she is passed from one to the other. Paul is pleased when English rather than French officers are their escorts as the French are rough and rude whereas the English are welcoming and friendly,

'Like gentlemen,' Paul says.

***

The *Arta* anchors in Constantinople bay on the 10th December at four in the morning. Paul comes on deck to a dreamlike vision. It is mild and warm, as they are used to in Odessa in May. There is a soft stillness in the air and the water laps gently against the sides of the ship. The city lies sleeping in a faint morning mist. This, the place of fairy tales and of a Thousand and One Nights. This, an oriental city with twinkling lights and candle-like minarets soaring into the sky. It is like a metamorphosis comparing this weather with the day before. The British frigate anchors close by, within hailing distance.

At eight o'clock, Paul sees two lighters approaching. One flies a French pennant, the other is British. Paul gathers that the French are in charge of the port arrangements here, while the British wish to ensure that all refugees arrive as planned at their final destination. The Frenchman informs the captain, with some disdain in his voice, that there will be thirteen more German refugees joining the ship. These arrive alongside very soon after the Englishman has followed the Frenchman on board. Paul looks casually down over the side at the waiting refugees crowded into the barge. They are the typical sad crowd of sorry refugees, wearing too many clothes (It is the easiest way to carry them.) They have bags of all shapes, colours and sizes. Whatever colour their clothing and bags started as it seems all have become a shade of dirty grey-green due to the rigours they have faced and the terrain they have endured. They are excited and talking loudly and quickly; curious as to how they will be received and what will be their fate. Paul watches these additional refugees being transferred to their ship and is idly wondering where they have come from and what trials they have faced. He spots three fair-haired children holding together. One a girl with pigtails. He looks again. What a surprise!

He shouts wildly and waves, 'Albert, Albert, Nellie!'

Sophia and the girls who have also been watching curiously but who have not noticed anything unusual, look first at Paul and then more intently below.

Then the girls also shout, 'Buba, Freddy, Mary.'

And Sophia, 'Nellie, Nellie look at me!' And waving, 'See here!' How are you?

The Frenchman does not approve of the excitement and tells the family to make less noise. The boarding party must be efficiently monitored and controlled as it comes on board. He instructs the freighter's captain to get his crew to control his passengers and to clear them from the boarding point. The Englishman gives Paul and family a smile and an understanding look. The two officials then stand side by side as the new refugees clamber on board, one by one. Both check the papers. The Frenchman already has a list of names and officiously ticks these off on his clipboard, as each refugee passes. The Englishman has no such record and must enter the names and other details in his ledger. This takes a little longer.

Both the Frenchman and the waiting refugees get impatient. The officials agree the refugees can all board but must wait in line until they have been checked-in. The crew corrals those waiting together on deck until their processing is complete. So the two families are close but not close enough to touch. There is much gesticulation, mouthing and lip-reading and jumping up and down by the younger generation.

Eventually, the checking is done, and the families reunite with a rush. There are hugs and kisses all round — nine excited family members all demanding three Russian kisses each, from all. Then there are the questions. They come faster than the answers, which tend to be long and complicated. It is a noisy, excited babble. The children separate from the grown-ups as they have different questions to ask. They find the grown-up talk too serious and boring. Already Tamara and Isa want to show their cousins round the ship, slightly to the concern of mother Cornelia but Sophia reassures her. Other passengers look on with sad smiles, perhaps thinking of the reunions that they would like to happen.

As soon as the registration procedure is completed the Frenchman leaves, giving instructions that the *Arta* must pull anchor within the next three hours. As the Englishman also prepares to leave Paul shakes his hand and thanks him for his understanding. He responds that it has made him happy to see the two families reunited.

The weather is good, so they find a place on the foredeck where they can sit and exchange experiences. Brother-in-law explains that he had seen that things were not going well for General Denikin and had decided that they had to escape. From his Cherson estate, it was convenient to get to the wool-exporting port of Nikolayev on the River Bug. From there, his connections had managed to find him a passage to Constantinople. He had been waiting for just over a week for the *Arta* to arrive. A big worry for him was that, while he had managed to bring quite a few belongings to Constantinople, those organising the *Arta* passage had said the family could only take what they could carry. He looks at his three children and says how good they have been, carrying loads almost as heavy as an adult's. He has left his remaining stuff with a trusted business friend but is dubious as to whether he will ever be able to retrieve it.

In the Dardanelles, they pass two sunken steamers with their masts sticking out of the water. They dock in Salonika and take on their last seven German refugees. In the Aegean, they experience a terrible storm. But in the Mediterranean, in the classic south, on the way to Gibraltar, they encounter the most enjoyable part of their journey, the most beautiful, the brightest and sunniest, calm weather. It gives pleasure to see the friendly green coast-line with the pretty little white Italian and Spanish houses. Near the Spanish border, they can see the snow-capped mountains. For part of the journey, they are close to Africa and see several small whirlwinds spiralling away over the coast and out of sight into the distance. It is so warm that they are on deck every day and taking saltwater showers in the middle of December.

Chapter 23 – Christmas Eve

The *Arta* arrives in Gibraltar on the 24th of December. The ship is quickly surrounded by small boats with Spaniards selling souvenirs and more interestingly, oranges, lemons, dates, peaches and sweet Mediterranean baklava. There is also the tender, manned by English sailors, bringing the officer in control on board to check with the captain. Once again, the girls are noticed and presented with chocolate. The German tradition is to celebrate on Christmas Eve, and all are looking forward to doing this peacefully in Gibraltar harbour.

The English show no pity on the refugee ship and force the *Arta* out of Gibraltar harbour into the wild Atlantic for Christmas Eve. Many think they have done this to spite the enemy. The escorting British frigate also has to ride the stormy seas, and there is some consolation and *Schadenfreude* (Pleasure in another's misfortune.) in that thought.

So the *Arta* and its passengers, with their improvised little Christmas tree, are thrown around like a small walnut shell. As there is no real tree, the passengers copy the sailors and search for the biggest broom they can find. They attach the handle of the broomstick to a bayonet and stick this into the table that hangs, like some of the beds, on four chains from the ceiling. They decorate the bristles with apples, mandarins, oranges and nuts. The foil from chocolate blocks serves as tinsel. Spaniards whose boats surrounded the *Arta* in Gibraltar sold them these luxuries. Finally, from somewhere, small candles appear. All surround the tree, and as it swings to and fro in the gale, they sing carols. There are many moist eyes, even amongst the men.

Isa tells – Christmas in Russia

In orthodox Russia, Christmas is not as big a feast as Easter, and the typical Christmas greeting is often *Snovom Godom* or Happy New Year. So we celebrated the German way.

But our first big Christmas treat was still Russian, and a week or two before we were taken to the children's matinee of the Nutcracker by Tchaikovsky. We usually travelled in a closed hired coach with the driver in blue livery. Mama and Mademoiselle came. Papa always said he was too busy. The theatre is beautiful, mostly gold and white with plush red seats and paintings on the ceiling and walls. We wore our best dresses and sat just a few rows from the front in the stalls. It was bustling, noisy, cheerful and exciting. There were many more children than grow-ups. We waved to friends from school sitting behind, in front and alongside us and shouted greetings to each other. Mademoiselle hushed us and instructed us to behave like ladies. When the lights went down, there was an immediate hush. Opera is usually for the grown-ups, but the Nutcracker is an exciting story, and we cheered and clapped as Clara helped the Nutcracker to defeat the wicked seven-headed mouse king. Next day back at home we would re-enact the play with our dolls. When, as usual, Tamara gave me the role of leading the mouse army, I found it very difficult to admit defeat, and our play often ended in an argument.

The last time we visited the Opera was in 1918 when the German army was in control of the town, and we saw, instead *Peterchens Mondfahrt* (Little Peter's Moon Journey - a favourite German fairy tale.)

On Christmas Eve we children were not allowed to see the decorated Christmas tree until after dark. Mama and Papa would disappear to the lounge. We would be confined to the nursery and listen to the bustling toing and froing in the hall. And from four o'clock onwards we would be pestering Mademoiselle that surely it was now dark enough. We were ready and impatient in our best dresses. At our last Christmas these had arrived just in time all the way from Vienna. They were white with broderie anglais edging, mine with a pink silk sash and Tamara's with pale blue.

At last, Papa would ring the little silver bell. It had once been my baby-rattle and had been Tamara's before that. We went with the story that the ringing was the sound of Father Christmas (or Father Frost, in Russian) departing with his reindeer after having left our presents. We dashed, our party shoes clicking on the polished wooden floor, to the living room to see the lighted tree. The magic and surprise were never less. The little burning candles swayed gently on the tree that reached high to the ceiling. Their flickering lights reflected in the various shaped and different coloured glass baubles. The pine smell. There were two wooden painted *Nussknacker* (nutcracker) soldiers, one in red the other in blue, guarding the presents under the tree.

It was a small family gathering, nothing like the bustle of Easter, including Oma and Mademoiselle Voutaz. Uncle Albert and Tante (German for Aunty) Tilla were usually also with us. They stayed two or three days and slept in the room to the right of the entrance that Mama made sure was always kept ready for their visits.

After the presents were all opened, we played with our new toys. Papa was then pressed to do *Bleigiessgiessen* (lit. Lead-pouring) For this, he first melted a scrap of lead in a large kitchen ladle over a candle, or two. The lead came either from Papa's car workshop or from our donation of a wounded lead toy-farm animal that missed leg or two. We debated whether an animal was sufficiently wounded to be sacrificed, but in our impatience to find some lead, we two tended to be rather brutal in offering up our handicapped animals. Papa then poured the bead of melted lead into cold water. It entered with a satisfying hiss and cooled into a distorted shape of silver-bright metal. This glinted in the light of the tree candles as it was fished out. We then begged Mama to tell the fortunes as each piece of lead was dropped wet and shiny, on to the waiting saucer. The fortunes depended on the contorted shapes that the metal formed and the creative imagination of the fortune-teller. We didn't want Papa doing the telling, as he liked to tease us with scary futures.

We were allowed to stay up and go to midnight service. This time to St Paul's, our own Lutheran evangelical church, which was not that far from the Orthodox Cathedral. However there was nothing like the gold decoration, the tinkling bells, icons and incense of the Orthodox but with its traditionally dressed Christmas tree and German carols, it had a unique atmosphere of its own. The smell was that of pine rather than incense. If we did go, Oma always insisted on wrapping us up warmly. She was convinced we would die of cold otherwise. She would shake the gloves on to our hands, pull our hats down firmly over our ears, crumpling them up as she did so, and make sure every button on our coats was fastened. As soon as we were outside, we would loosen our collars and get comfortable again. However, on more than one occasion, by the time it was to leave, one or both of us would have fallen asleep. If so, either Oma or Mademoiselle Voutaz stayed behind to look after us. Next morning we would be teased.

***

Two days out of Gibraltar the *Arta* hits the Bay of Biscay. The Bay leaves no one on board in doubt that its reputation is deserved. Huge waves, such as can only occur in big oceans, batter the little ship. These follow one after another, like an unending chain of high mountains. These waves are almost the end of Paul. Together with his cache of preserved meats, bacon and sausages he has brought a small frying pan and is going to the little galley on deck to cook when he realises that a massive wave is descending upon the *Arta* and on him. He only just manages to grab the safety line that surrounds the deck with his left hand but holds onto the frying pan with his right in the hope that the wave will merely pass over him. But as the wave breaks, he realises that one hand is not going to be enough and, although it hurts, lets go of his pan with its precious contents and quickly grabs the line with both hands. As the wave engulfs him, he sees the pan's contents disappear into the waves. He ruefully hopes that the fish will enjoy their extra treat. Luckily the pan somehow gets caught among some ship's chains, and he can retrieve it. So he rinses and refills it and this time manages to finish his chef's task.

Poor Sophia suffers severe seasickness in the terrible weather while the rest of the family is much less affected. The captain takes pity and allows her to rest in his cabin when she is so unwell. She is even given the use his toilet which is an even greater kindness. The public facilities on board the little freight ship have become a nauseous, messy nightmare, with over half the passengers urgently seeking out a place in which to vomit.

Chapter 24 – Hamburg

The freighter arrives in Plymouth to bunker and take on provisions on the first day of 1920. Looking over the railings, Paul breathes a deep sigh of relief, nearly home – a new beginning in a new year. It appears that there is a crew change on the naval escort vessel as he can see many sailors getting on and off[18]. There are families on the dockside waving and greeting the sailors as they disembark.

The expected visit and inspection by a naval officer takes place. He is as polite and civil, as his earlier countrymen had been, and wishes them a safe journey home. After just a single night's stay, they are sailing on the last leg of their journey. The expectations and excitement mixed with uncertainty as to their reception are high.

*****

On the 6th January 1920, the *Arta* enters the wide mouth of the River Elbe. Before reaching Hamburg proper, she ties-up at Brunnsbütel where the refugees are overwhelmed to be greeted with a brass band, speeches of welcome and the glorious smell and taste of real, fresh coffee that is brought on board for them. However an unpleasant surprise also awaits.

---

[18] They were probably docked in Devonport, the Naval dockyard of Plymouth and the home-port of several of the naval vessels active in the 1919 Odessa Operation.

They are instructed to disembark and herded into a large warehouse. They are shocked as Medical orderlies, in white overalls and with masks, separate the men from the women and children. Once separated a greater shock follows. This is the order to undress – completely! And to place their clothing in the sacks provided. The sacks have labels attached, on which to write names. This results in a frantic search for pencils. Only after persistent questioning does Sophia learn that this is a compulsory delousing procedure. They are next directed into a smoke filled fumigation room. The acrid fumes catch the back of the throat and there is a frantic coughing and a waving of hands in front of faces, both to dispel the fumes and also to see better. Julia, who does not seem to be quite as badly affected as some, comments to Sophia what a beautiful figure the young woman, just in front of them in the mist, has. Sophia agrees without really looking. She is more concerned with not losing sight of Tamara and Isa. Tamara appraises the young beauty, looks down at herself and decides that she will look just like that in a few years time.

After ten minutes they are directed into another large room with benches around the wall and told to wait for their clothes. Now, with the excitement less, they notice the January cold. Some are exhausted and in spite of the cold sit on the benches. Others crowd round one of the three coal-burning fires that are arranged in a line down the centre of the hall. But most simply stand and shiver with their arms clasped in front of themselves. Eventually assistants enter carrying the bags of clothing. The bags without names are piled onto trestles at the end of the room and owners invited to search for their belongings. There is a rush. Two other assistants start to read out the names on the labels that have been completed. Sophia did have a pencil and had managed to fill-in her name, and had squeezed all their clothes into a single bag. The name of Vaatz is eventually called. Tamara and Isa charge through the crowd to collect it. The clothes feel warm and damp, as they disentangle them, and Sophia wonders how they have been disinfected. Isa the first to discover that some items have shrunk. Her woollen gloves would now better fit her doll.

Paul has been waiting for some time before the ladies of his entourage emerge. He like them is wearing very rumpled clothing. His theory is that the clothes have been through a steaming process to kill the lice. Sophia remains highly offended that anyone would think that she carried a single louse.

Following the grand reception and the less than grand delousing experience they are allowed to re-embark and sail on to the centre of the city. The *Arta* births at Dock Number 5. Here they are yet again received with a brass band and good-will speeches. Although Paul and Sophia know that these warm welcomes are intended mainly for the brave soldiers returning home, it still makes them both feel wanted and happy to be 'home.'

As they prepare to disembark, Paul hands his bag of valuables to Tamara to hold, and then gathers her and Isa, one under each arm. He walks slowly and proudly down the gangplank with them. Sophia follows content to see Paul so happy and proud of his girls. She places a hand on his shoulder for balance, as she looks down and negotiates the wooden strips of the gang-plank. He breathes in the fresh air of freedom and safety. He marvels how from 1914 these two young things had battled through the repeated dangers they faced together and never complained. What brave, sensible girls they are. In these five years they have matured from little girls to young ladies. Tamara will be a fourteen-year-old teenager later this year, and Isa ten next month. He wants to cry with relief at them all having escaped the vicious hell that Odessa has become. His daughters must have a safe and happy future.

Before leaving the dock, Sophia dashes off to buy a small doll in the harbour souvenir shop for the captain who has been so kind. He had mentioned that he too had a daughter two years younger than Isa. He is clearly touched when Isa and Tamara present him with this little gift.

The family had fled Odessa on the 6th December and finally arrived at their new home on the 6th January. Exactly one month. On route, they had docked at Constantinople, Salonika, Gibraltar and Plymouth. It was said on board that theirs was the last journey of the 5,000-ton steamer that the English would allow to sail under a German flag. She had rescued Paul's family from the Red-Bolshevik hell-hole and brought them all safely to their Motherland. Paul gives the ship a final look and thanks her silently for the peaceful, safe asylum they had all received from her for a whole month. She is to be requisitioned, and from now, she will serve their most bitter enemies.

Paul and Sophia used to visit Europe and especially Hamburg, most years. Tamara was even born there in 1906. These visits were partly to retain their German citizenship. Sophia can't help thinking how happy and carefree they had been then. In those days they were at home in Russia, in Germany, and much of Europe. Now they are refugees! But both Paul and Sophia realise that they are lucky refugees as they have good friends in the city who have invited them to stay, as long as they wished, until they can decide what to do. Paul orders a taxi to the Innen Alster. It is a luxury that they cannot really afford. But they are desperate and very tired. Their friends expect them but do not know when. Nevertheless the welcome they receive, when they ring the bell can be no warmer nor more sympathetic and concerned.

'How are you? You must be hungry, you must be tired. Do you want a bath? Your beds are all ready.'

The girls receive special hugs and kisses.

These friends seemed to Tamara, on their visits in earlier days, to be very rich. Their hosts used paper roubles as book-marks or lost money in the furniture. Tamara remembers how she and Isa used to riffle through the books and search under the cushions for any stray money. They could only do this, secretly, when Mama and Papa were not around. On this visit they have time for only one quick search, as after only two days Paul is offered a post with Mercedes in Stuttgart based on his successful representation of the company in Odessa. The girls do, 'by chance' find ten roubles under the cushions. These they properly present to their host. He, as they had hoped, says they must keep them. This is in spite of Papa's embarrassment and objections.

The German authorities are well organised to receive their fellow ethnic refugees, and the family is issued with a Red-Cross voucher giving them free rail passage to Stuttgart. Albert Linke, Nellie and children travel with Paul's family on to Stuttgart. They all have one primary concern, and that is for Albert and Mathilde. Why had they been so obstinate, so stupid? And, as time passes and the news of how things are developing in Odessa worsens, their worries increase.

Chapter 25 – Last Chance

Paul and family are very fortunate to have departed in good order on that last German-captained ship. How very lucky becomes clear only two months later when Odessa is again overwhelmed. This time it is not through invasion by a regular Red Army force but by an uprising of agitators inside the city. This disintegrates into an uncontrolled looting and the murderous rout of the town. It is an uprising that, commentators said, a coordinated military response could have quickly put down. But the White officers, instead of holding-on to protect their city, decided to flee, and in this, they were lead by their commanding officer, General Schilling.

On that night, 5 February 1920 Albert and Mathilde, are woken by the sound of shooting. Through the windows, they can see fires a few streets away. It is time to leave. They each stuff a bag of essentials, Albert is telling Mathilde to hurry. Two small packs of valuables are already prepared. They open the door of their temporary accommodation, close to St Pauls Evangelical Cathedral, uncertain which way to run as there are fires and shooting, it seems, in all directions. However, they join the bulk of other frightened residents running, or walking as fast as they can, down Peter the Great Street towards the harbour. They cross through Ekaterininskaya Square and continue to the top of the Potemkin steps above the port, where they put down their bags tired and frightened.

They stand close, looking down at the chaotic mix of noise, movement and flashing lights in the darkness below. A vicious cold wind is blowing, carrying flakes of snow. They descend into the melee and push their way backwards and forwards along the quayside trying to find a lighter willing to take them out to the rescue ships anchored in the harbour. But each one is full or will take only Greeks, only French or only White officers. They become exhausted and dispirited and huddle together on a cold stone wall. Mathilde, being the perfect wife, has thought to bring food and they sit chewing, sausage in one hand and dry rye bread in the other, watching the chaos and wondering what to do. Morning is breaking, and it is getting lighter, which raises their spirits a little as they can see better and understand more clearly what is happening. The gunfire is definitely getting closer. Just opposite them on the quay a lighter ties up. A shout goes out for Russians needing to leave. Albert gets up.

'Don't be silly, Albert. We're Germans.'

'Today, we are still Russian.' Albert responds and adds, 'Perhaps for the last time. Come on.' He pulls her from her seat.

A desperate crowd already overwhelms the landing stage. Albert pushes forward and sees, over the shoulders of those pressing in front, that papers are being checked and that some are being turned away in spite of pleas for mercy. He falters, but just then there are gun-shots, and the sharp sound of metal being struck. Someone at the back screams they have been hit. There is panic. Checking papers is forgotten, speed is all that matters. Albert and Mathilde are pushed forward and are suddenly on board.

There is a splash, a scream and a shout of 'Saskia!

At least one victim has been sacrificed to the freezing water as the lighter pushes off. Others, both those stranded on the quayside and those barely on-board, are only just saved from also being lost, as the gangplank is hauled into the moving boat. It is severely overloaded, and a loud shout goes out, not all to stand on one-side. Those lucky enough to have got on board are straining to see what they are leaving behind. The firing becomes unbelievingly rapid.

Onshore there is a desperate scatter to find shelter. On board, all crouch low and many pray.

Someone says, 'Good God. They've got machineguns now....... Poor devils.'

The early, scattered flakes of snow in the wind develop into a blinding blizzard as they arrive at a Russian warship. Those terrible machineguns that were firing at them as they fled are now out of range. The transfer operation is not simple, as they have to jump from the bobbing lighter on to a ladder strung down the grey side of the warship. The wind and blizzard do not make it easier. They cannot see properly, especially Paul, with his short-sightedness. Fingers are cold, and grip is uncertain. Luckily both have bags they can sling over their shoulders and so have their hands free to scale the wood-runged rope ladder. Those with suitcases or, even worse, boxes, have to leave them in the lighter and hope that they will be hauled up after them. Albert and Mathilde balance themselves in the lighter as two, unable to climb, are hoisted up, in turn, in a breeches buoy. One is holding a pair of crutches, crossed untidily, close to his chest. It is a very ungainly and uncomfortable looking procedure, as he swings to and fro on his way up. Two sailors, who Albert notices immediately are officers, help the fugitives in over the side. In spite of the sleet and the cold, the mood is almost jolly because of the relief of escape.

The lighter, they learn, and the warship itself is manned solely by Russian officers, the crew having either mutinied, deserted or been shot. In spite of the sleet and wind, Albert and Mathilde settle on the lea side of the deck under the bridge. Sophia refuses to go below in case the ship is sunk. But then nothing happens. The boat does not move. At first, they do not notice, as they are more concerned with observing the horror taking place onshore and are relieved not to be part of it. Then the news starts to circulate that the ship has no power. Albert wonders whether this is lack of fuel, a technical fault, or just that the officers do not know how to fire up the engines. Will they have to return to Odessa and the carnage in the harbour?

H.M.S. CERES.

HMS Ceres

A British warship comes alongside. Beware the enemy! Is Albert's first thought. There is a loudhailer exchange between the two captains – with replies from the Russian captain in a broken but understandable English. After much manoeuvring and the throwing across of hawsers, Albert and Mathilde realise they are moving. The British cruiser *HMS Ceres*, with its two steaming funnels and cannons fore and aft, is towing them! To where? The journey is hard and uncomfortable. There is nowhere to sleep, and it is icy cold. They compare fingers to determine whose are the whiter. But Mathilde will still not go below. It is even more crowded down there than on deck. So they do their best to keep each other warm. They have heavy coats and waterproof winter clothing but still move twice during the night to find better shelter from the wind blowing across the decks.

As they sit close, shivering in the cold, Albert curses himself for the decisions he has made. If he had had his way, he and Mathilde would have been almost the first out of Russia and heading for Germany. When the German troops occupied the Ukraine in early 1918, he had decided it would be a good, peaceful time to leave. With a friendly army in control, there would be no difficulty in getting to the Motherland. He could always return if and when the situation settled. He had already started to pack and to decide what to ship ahead when the German occupying force appeared and located their command post at his Karlovka estate. On hearing of Albert's plans, the general whom he was hosting, politely asked him to remain. Although phrased as a request, it was really an order. The general feared that, if Albert fled, the smaller farmers would follow. Germany desperately needed the food supplies that the farmers could provide. Albert's second mistake, of course, was not to leave on the *Arta* with his brother. The silly reason, this time, being that because of the chaos in the countryside, he had been unable to prepare and would have had to leave so much behind. Now he and Mathilde had, in any case, lost almost everything.

The crew of officers somehow manages to produce a small portion of soup for all on the first evening. It is clearly a mix. Mathilde assumes they have just thrown everything they could find in the storeroom into the pot. They are fed in shifts, and bowls and spoons are not washed before being reused, not just once but two or three times. No one complains. It is warming and very welcome. On the second day, which is sunny although still cold, they watch the skilful transfer of stores from the *Ceres*, using lines thrown between the two vessels. As a result of this, they assume, they receive another serving of soup on the second evening. It is a good, proper soup and someone suggests it must have been made with the famous English beef. It comes, also, with a thick slice of strange white English bread.

Albert hears whisperings in both Greek and Yiddish and realises that he and Mathilde are not the only non-ethnic Russians who had scrambled on board in the Odessa harbour panic. In this crisis of life and death all are equal, he decides. He and Mathilde speak only Russian together. No point in complicating the situation and inviting questions.

On the afternoon of the third day, they arrive at the Bulgarian port of Varna. This is the closest port, west of Odessa, at which they can disembark. Romania, which would have provided an earlier landfall, is not accepting refugees.

Albert thanks the Russian captain, as they disembark the crippled ship and he asks him to pass sincere thanks to the British captain of the *Ceres* which has towed them on their journey to safety.

As Mathilde also thanks the captain, she asks him what he and his fellow officers will do now. Even if he can get his ship's engines going again, he can hardly return to Odessa.

'Ah, dear, kind lady, I will probably go to France. I speak the language and, as an ally, they might give me a job in their navy. My big worry, though, is how to get my wife and children out of that hell.'

'Thank you again,' and she pats, with her left hand, the hand she is shaking, 'And good luck with your family.'

As they walk down the gangplank Albert acknowledges to Mathilde that the British have done them a great favour, possibly even saving their lives.

Stuttgart is still 2000 km away, a journey made longer than otherwise because of the need to avoid Romania and its uncompromising refugee policy. They go via Sofia, Belgrade, Budapest, Vienna and Munich. They find Austria in turmoil following the collapse of the Austro-Hungarian Empire. In November 1918 Austria had agreed to join with Germany and renamed itself German-Austria. But already in September 1919, they were forced by the allies to repudiate that act and to become a separate state. Both the administration and businesses remain in a confused state of readjustment. The postage stamps that Albert sticks on his postcards to Paul in Stuttgart still carry the Deutsch-Österreich (German-Austria) name.

Albert and Mathilde follow the Danube where they can and use a mixture of regular passenger ferries and by negotiating passage on heavy-goods barges. The river option is perhaps slower but seems surer and is less tiring than worrying with train timetables and changing stations. Albert manages to send a telegram from Vienna to say they are on their way.

There is an emotional reunion between the two brothers and two sisters when Albert and Mathilde arrive in Stuttgart. Tamara and Isa scream with joy at seeing their favourite aunt and uncle again and rush at them with open arms.

As Albert takes Paul's welcoming hand, he says, 'I can see what you are thinking young brother, and I admit you were right, so, so right. We should have left with you.'

Paul just hugs him close, pats him firmly on the back, and murmurs, 'Thank God, thank Almighty God, you're both safe.'

Epilogue

Paul's position in Stuttgart that he is given so quickly after his arrival is terminated with regrets by Mercedes within less than a year. His dismissal reference makes clear that this is due to the depression of the twenties and the resulting lack of business that is affecting all of Europe.

While the family is suffering the depression in Germany, Paul and Sophia are nevertheless aware of the hardships and starvation that are ravaging the villages in the Odessa region through which they had fled. They feel immense gratitude and a great sadness towards the modest but brave villagers who had, so often, risked their lives to save his family and enable them to escape to safety. As Sophia had predicted, standing on the deck of the *Arta* watching Odessa disappear, she never did see her mother again. There is a sad message in a postcard carrying communist stamps, in 1920, from a carer who explains how her mother is failing and now needs a great deal of help.

Paul and Sophia rent a largish house at Teckstrasse, 52 in Backnang, a suburb of Stuttgart. To earn some income, they let the spare rooms. The five young sons of a London hotel owner visit in twos and threes to learn the language. Two of these court and marry Tamara and Isa, respectively – another union of two brothers with two sisters. Both couples settle in London.

In the late twenties, Paul eventually receives compensation via the German government from funds that the Bolsheviks agreed to pay for the properties confiscated in Russia. Only land is compensated for. Movable property is not included. Although the sum obtained is only a small percentage of the value of what they have lost, they are still able to buy a small farm near Berlin. The plan of his Schastlivka estate, which he had protected so carefully during the flight, aided considerably in proving his right to compensation. The family later sell the farm and settle in southern Germany.

Considering what remains of the past, the Marazlievskaya apartment, although divided in half, is being well used. When we visited in 2018, one side was being professionally refurbished to a high standard. The park opposite is, I imagine, as beautiful as our ancestors saw it. Perhaps more so as the trees will have matured in those hundred years. The Catherine the Great monument that we admired and assumed was the original, I discover is not. Hiding it in wrappings, as Paul had experienced, was not sufficient for the Bolsheviks. It was torn down in 1920 and replaced with a monument to the sailors of the Potemkin. In 1995 the town council made plans to restore the Catherine statue using pieces preserved in the museum. However, the then president of the Ukraine blocked the plans. A restored monument was eventually completed in 2007 together with a full refurbishing of the whole square. However, in the newly independent Ukraine it remains controversial with some wanting to have the monument torn down, again.

Grossliebental, although the name is now changed to Velikodolyns'ke, is in good shape with its traditional colony houses being upgraded and well looked after. The former Lutheran church that in Stalin times had been reduced to a cow-shed is now a beautifully restored as an Orthodox church. The Karlovka estate is derelict and not in use with trees and brush growing through decaying outbuildings, barns and the ice-house. The main house was obviously demolished, again probably in the Stalin era, but it has since been rebuilt on the old foundations as an Orthodox church. This has an unusually fine avenue of trees leading to it for a village church – a remnant of the grand farm estate. Not even derelict buildings are left on the Schastlivka site, although the dam depicted on the plan, while silted up and poorly maintained, is still there, complete with white geese. The graveyard shown on the map exists. However, we could find no graves from pre-revolutionary times.

There are two Vaatzs in the family tree who do not appear in this account. Louise, Paul's second oldest sibling, is never mentioned in the family sagas. Perhaps she died early. Emil, the second youngest is spoken of, but in tones of horror. He married and had two children. Unlike Paul, in 1914 he was interned in the far north and apparently suffered greatly. When allowed home he went 'mad,' left his family, became ultra religious, gave away all his land and finally committed suicide.

There were two Kunderts. One, the brother of Sophia and Mathilde was also interned but following his release he managed to emigrate to Germany and to continue life as an artist. The other Waldemar, whose link with the family is less clear, became a highly regarded engineer and architect. He has the distinction of, in 1904, supervising the mounting the canon of a British frigate, the HMS Tiger as a war trophy outside the City Hall. This was on the 50th anniversary of the frigate's sinking by the Odessa battery after it had grounded while bombarding the town on the way to the Crimean war in 1854. He was one of the few that coped with the change of regime, remained in Odessa, and established himself as an expert in the growing field of reinforced concrete structures.

The Odessa samovar. It is still cherished and fired up at Easter. The author with Ukrainian friend, Irina. [Photo: Oksana Zbyranyk]

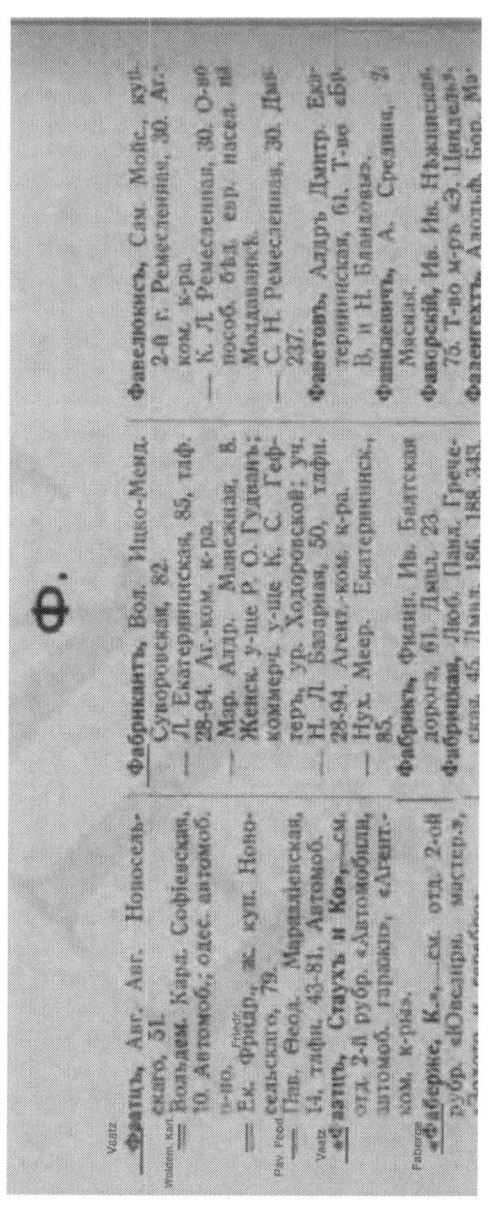

Fabergé. It's interesting to see that, under F (Cyrillic Ф) in the 1914 edition of the *Odessa Gazette* that the various Vaatz (Pronounced Faatz) enterprises are listed immediately above Fabergé, and to know that the family sometimes ate with Fabergé silver.

Tailpiece

Thank you for reading this memoire. I hope you found it interesting and learned something new. Do please submit a review and rate it on Amazon. It helps to spread the news.

Apparently you have to have spent at least $50 on Amazon in the last 12 months in order to qualify as a reviewer. To review go to:

www.Amazon.co.uk or www.amazon.com

Search for the **Odessa 1919** book with Ronald French as author.

Above the book's image will appear: *You purchased his item on xxx* and *View this order*.

Click *View this order*. On the right you will see options. Fifth down is:

Write a product review

Click once more and write your review.

Thank you.

It is easy to amend both Ebooks and paper-backs, even following publication. You are always welcome to email me with errors and comments. In a historical biography it is important to get the facts right.

RonaldFrench1919@icloud.com

FREE

Karlovka, you will remember is important to the story, as this is where the two girls spent many happy summer months. It is also where Uncle Albert was forced to remain when wanting to run from the Red Terror. The German occupation forces needed him to continue farming to provide essential food for a starving Germany. If you would like to know how we rediscovered the family farm estates of Schastlivka and Karlovka. You will find an informal account, with photographs on the Black Sea German Research website at:

http://www.blackseagr.org/pdfs/Karlovka-rediscovery-French_Ron.pdf.

If you would like to know more about our research in Odessa and the German colony villages, email me and I shall find a way to put these other accounts on the web as well.

List of Illustrations

Cover From: *In the basements of the Cheka* by Ivan Vladimirov, 1919.

['Public Domain' https://www.rbth.com/history/329091-how-many-lives-claimed-red-terror%5D . Permission requested 21/8/2019

Frontispiece The Khodinka beaker

Prologue Paul and family, 1914

War Bonds

Vaatz family tree

Plan of Odessa

Map of villages & estates

Chapter 1 The Ukrainian Paska

All in the Mercedes

Chapter 2 Mercedes showroom 1914

[Mercedes-Benz Classic Archive]

Chapter 3 Inauguration of Catherine II monument 1900

[File:Opening of the monument to Catherine the Great in Odessa.jpg. (2017, January 28). Wikimedia Commons, the free media repository. Retrieved 17:42, September 18, 2019 From https://bit.ly/33s9YiR.]

Victorious Austro-Hungarian troops, 1918.

[Österreichisches Staatsarchiv, Operative Kriegsführung http://wk1.staatsarchiv.at]

	May Day, 1919.

[Sergey Kotelko: http://sergekot.com/ekaterininskaya-ploshhad/]
Permission requested 18/9/2019

Chapter 4	Holy Trinity picnic, 1901
Chapter 5	Ladies day at the Odessa Automobile Club.
Chapter 6	Marazlievskaya 14b, 2018
Chapter 8	Flight from the CheKa, map
Chapter 9	Grossliebental – cemetery visit

[Homesteaders on the Steppe by Joseph S. Height, p332-333]

Chapter 15	Mercedes Workshop, 1912

[Mercedes-Benz Classic Archive]

Chapter 16	Saved from barter
Chapter 17	Schastlivka land plan
	Karlovka tower
	On the Karlovka steps, 1914
	Red beard & Karlovka view
	The Karlovka yard
Chapter 21	House of Torture, 1919. [The Times, 1919]
Chapter 22	Uncle Carl & Oma at Schastlivka
Chapter 25	HMS Ceres, 1920.

[Gordon Smith: Naval-history.net/PhotoWW1-06clCeres1PS.jpg]

Epilogue	The Odessa Samovar
Tailpiece	Vaatz and Fabergé

Every effort has been made to find the source and to seek permission from potential image copyright holders. The sources, where known are indicated. However, as the events described are at least 100 years old I trust no infringements have occurred.

Acknowledgements

I thank all the family members who have encouraged and supported me in my research and in the writing of this historical memoire. I am especially grateful to those who accompanied me on one or both of our visits to Odessa and its surrounds. My mother, Isa who was with us on our first visit was very good at recalling the happy memories and in telling us the bad ones, more as adventures than as disasters. On that first visit in 1999, when she was 89, she charmed the Russians whom we met; first, those in the little orchestra on the steamship, Lavrinenkov on which we sailed to Odessa along the River Dnieper from Kiev. They happily played all her favourite Russian tunes. Then there were the three generations, Irina, Galinya and Anya, living in one half of the flat Isa's family had owned in 1919, whom we visited without warning. On the following day, as we went to the Opera, the three ladies were waiting for her at the entrance with flowers and gifts. The family members with me on the first visit were Isa, Peter, Felicity, Martha, Emma and Tim.

While we learned what we could during that first visit, the second visit, in 2018, was for serious research, as I planned to publish the story of the family's escape during its 100th anniversary year, 2019. We comprised of three generations. Cousin Dorothy helped to solve the conundrum in which, all the published evidence gave Carl Vaatz as the owner of the Schastlivka estate, whereas my evidence was that his brother Paul was the owner. The simple resolution was that both had inherited a portion of the estate when their father died. Dorothy also retrieved original historical material held by her sister Nancy in San Francisco. These documents were particularly useful in understanding Paul's founding of the Odessa Mercedes dealership and confirming where in the city the workshop was located. Those contributing to the 2018 visit were Peter, Paul, Dorothy, Carolyn, Sarah, Emma, James, Sophia, Guy, Poppy and George.

Drs Fritz & Gisela Baukloh-Lajosi, family members through a female line, showed great interest in the research, provided an extended family tree of the Vaatz family plus many carefully annotated historical photographs, new to me. In researching the Vaatz name, I discovered Arnold Vaatz, member of the German Bundestag and a minister of the CDU, and informed him of my interest. Although our respective family branches separated already in the early 1820s, he generously forwarded me a beautifully presented, Excel-based, family tree. I have adapted a small portion of this for the Prologue.

I am fortunate in having received the advice of three professional editors. Amanda Bourn, Production Editor, the Scottish Provincial Press, very generously offered valuable editorial comment. Diana Collis of Jericho Writers provided further editing, comments and advice. Penny James-Lucas generously presented me with a fully annotated manuscript with corrections and suggestions. Brothers Peter and Paul, cousins John and Douglas, niece Sarah and nephew Khaldoon, amongst others also identified typos and omissions.

I thank Dr Joseph Drew, an academic friend of many years standing, and editor of the Comparative Civilisations Review that published the first version of this memoire, for his encouragement. He gave me the confidence that the project was worth progressing, which resulted in my 1918 research visit.

Among other friends was Chris Thomas, who used her Russian to extract pearls of interest from the extensive collection of postcards that my mother had assembled almost from birth. Other friends with experience, patience and honest advice included Sheila Preston, Alexia Fairweather, Lynn Eden and Lucy Johnson. Bob Tilney, weapons expert and presenter in the Antiques Road Show, kindly commented on my accounts of the use of weapons.

The US-based Black Sea German Research web site was a particularly valuable resource that was made even more so by the personal interest shown, and the support rendered by Gayla Aspenleiter and Carolyn Schott. A particular triumph was to determine the precise location of the Karlovka estate, which no longer appears on modern maps. They kindly arranged for the informal family record of our re-discovery of Karlovka to be placed on the Black Sea German Research website at: http://www.blackseagr.org/pdfs/Karlovka-rediscovery-French_Ron.pdf

My visit to the Hamburg archives, searching through difficult to read microfilmed records, was made much more fruitful than it might have been due to the support and expert advice of Barbara Köschlig. Email correspondence with Wolfgang Rabus, Beate Frank and Daniela Sigl of the Mercedes Archives in Stuttgart provided photographs and vital information regarding the interaction between Paul in Odessa and the Mercedes headquarters in Stuttgart and helped to confirm the location of the showroom and workshop in Odessa. And I am grateful to the management for allowing me to include archive photographs.

On our visit to the apartment at 14b Marazlievskaya in 2018, Larisa Serafimovna and her son Ivanov Vladyslav kindly welcomed us with tea and biscuits. This was particularly interesting for those of us who had been on the first visit, as we gained entry to the other half of the original larger apartment. In particular, we were able to look out of the kitchen window and to reimagine the episode in which the family valuables were lowered down into the yard, in a shopping basket, to smuggle them past the Red Guards.

In Grossliebental we could not get into the original Kundert house as it was locked. However, the German colony village houses all have a very similar basic structure and Yulia, and Dmitriy Berizov invited us to explore their home, close-by. One new thing we learned was that these houses had generous cellars, cut into the limestone upon which they stood, and of which they were also built.

We were supported throughout the visit by Serge Ehlias who acted as researcher, guide and interpreter. He extracted evidence from the Odessa archives, including the addresses of various members of the Kundert and Vaatz families in Odessa, and confirmed that a Vaatz had been interned in the Cheka and then released. Between us we realised that Paul's Schadanov Building (spelt the German way) and Serge's Zhdanov Building (spelt the Russian way) were one and the same, so confirming that the CheKa headquarters was located at 6 Ekaterininaskya Square, directly opposite Paul's Mercedes showroom. Serge helped with the naming of streets, many of which had experienced at least three changes since the start of World War I. He guided us through Odessa and, more importantly, during our extended trek through the villages, and eventually to our discoveries at the two former family estates 150 km to the north of Odessa.

Sources

The structure of this memoire is based on the typewritten and annotated account by Paul Vaatz of his family's traumatic last nine months in Russia, fleeing arrest and execution by the Odessa Bolshevik CheKa. The handwritten and verbal evidence of his two daughters Tamara and Isa supplement his story. They have also passed on descriptions of events as told to them by their mother, aunt and grandmother. Annotated photographs, postcards and ephemera have helped to provide detail.

    A visit was made to Odessa and its environs in 1999, together with Paul's daughter, Isa who was 89 at the time. This included being invited into the old family apartment overlooking Alexander Park. A longer research visit was made in 2018. All streets mentioned in the text have been walked and the many apartments where members of the extended family lived, viewed. The route of the family's flight, through the German colony villages, was retraced. Two of the family's, now derelict, country farming-estates that are mentioned in the story, were discovered and explored. Accounts of the visits have been recorded within the family but have not so far been made public (Except for one. See Acknowledgements and Tailpiece.) Before the second research visit, an earlier version of the family's flight was published in the Comparative Civilizations Review.

The literature and history of World War I and the revolutionary period have been researched to confirm event dates and pre-revolutionary place names. The archives of Odessa, Hamburg and Mercedes have revealed valuable information. A shortlist of the main sources is given below.

Eisfeld, A. (September 2003) *200 Jahre Ansiedlung der Deutschen im Schwarzmeergebie*t [200 years of settlement by the Germans in the Black Sea region] Lecture presented in Neuenschloss, Stuttgart. Includes a table (p11) showing which forces held power in Odessa during the period 1917 to 1920. Some of the dates in Paul Vaatz's account (see below) are somewhat vague, and this listing is helpful.

French (nee Vaatz,) sisters Tamara and Isa. Extensive verbal communication over the years. Handwritten manuscripts in German and English of life in Odessa before and during the Revolution, as experienced themselves and as narrated to them by her mother, mother's sister and maternal grandmother. Also a collection of postcards received from family members and friends dating from 1912 to well after 1920. Understandably, no cards date from the period of the flight.

Geschichte der Russlanddeutschen [History of the Russian-Germans]
Auswanderung der Deutschen Teil III 1917 - 1955
1. Die Oktoberrevolution und ihre Auswirkungen auf die Russlanddeutschen
1.7 Kampf um die Sicherung der bolschewistischen Macht in den Jahren 1918 bis 1920
1.7.1 Russlanddeutsche im Bürgerkrieg
1.7.1.1 Banden/Bürgerkrieg in der Ukraine (This section provides useful detail on the Grossliebental battle of the villages between 20 July and 12 August 1919.)

Available at http://www.russlanddeutschegeschichte.de/geschichte/teil3/revolution/banden.htm (Accessed 8 January 2019)

Hamburger Korrespondenz (7 January 1920) Newspaper evidence that the steamship *Arta* docked in Hamburg on 5 January 1920 – interestingly, Paul's account says the 6th. (Last date in dock is recorded as 29 January.) Paul says that the ship was handed over to the British as war reparations. I could find no supporting evidence for this. Accessed in Hamburg Archives, 2018.

Hornet Info (No date) Pamphlet describing the origins of Marazlievkaya and its houses, their architects and owners. Available at https://www.hor.net.ua/?page_id=1149&lang=en (Accessed 2 April 2019)

Kotelko, Serge, (No date) *Екатерининская площадь Дом 6. Доходный дом Ждановой.* [Ekaterininskaya Square. House 6, Zhdanov Apartments] This study of the development of the Zhdanov building provides incidental but interesting detail regarding the Catherine the Great monument. Available at http://sergekot.com/ekaterininskaya-ploshhad/ (Accessed 8 April 2019)

Liebrandt, George (1939) *Quellen zur Erforschung des Deutschtums in Osteuropa* [Source for the study of German influence in Eastern Europe] S. Hirzel, Leipzig. In three volumes. Provides details of the government, farming management and business activities in the German colony villages in the 19th and early 20th centuries. Johann Kundert (Sophia's father) is mentioned numerous times.

Linke, Bubi (1994) *Episodes from the country of my ancestors*, Speech by Bubi Linke (Son of Buba,) Eichstätt, Germany. The Linkes were Vaatz descendants on the female side, and the two families were close. Bubi's is a two-page account of the traumas the Linke family experienced during 1919. His story broadly supports and supplements the Vaatz version but in detail sometimes contradicts it. There is a particular confusion in stories relating to 'Albert' between Albert Vaatz, Paul's oldest brother, and Albert Linke, husband of Paul's sister, Cornelia (Nellie.) I have presented the Vaatz version. After the second world war, the Linke family migrated still further west, to San Francisco, to be as far away from Communism as possible.

Odessa Operation (1919) A good account of the retaking of Odessa by General Denikin's forces on the 23rd July, including the part played by the British cruiser Caradoc. Available at: https://en.wikipedia.org/w/index.php?title=Odessa_Operation_(1919)&oldid=909004722. (Accessed 1 July 2019) It is a translation of the original Russian Wiki available at: https://ru.wikipedia.org/wiki/Одесская_операция_(1919). The latter is a longer article with better quality illustrations and providing primary sources.

Rabus, Wolfgang and Frank, Beate (2018) Private communication, Archivists, Mercedes–Benz, Classic Archive, Stuttgart. Provided photographs of Odessa showroom and workshop in 1914 and the name of the manager at the time, and also a copy of Paul's terminating job reference, showing that he was given a position with Mercedes but only from 1 February to 30 September 1920. Signed by Hoenemer, 1920.

Stumpp, Karl (1955) *Karte der deutschen Siedlungen im gebiet Odessa: ehem. westl. Teil des Gouv. Cherson, Stand 1940*, Publ. Stumpp [Map of German settlements in the Odessa region: formerly: Gouvernement of West Cherson, situation in 1940.] This locates the German villages and farm estates mentioned in Paul's narrative.

Stumpp, Karl (No date) *Die Geschichte der Familie Vaatz, Schwarzmeergebiet, Kreis Ananiew* [History of the Vaatz family, Black Sea region, Ananiev county] Copy of a newspaper or journal article presenting the growth in ownership of land by the Vaatz family and its increase in value. His figures mirror the handwritten notes of Albert Vaatz (below) that are almost certainly the original source. The date and journal in which this article appears are not indicated.

Tucker, S. C. (Ed) (1996) *The European Powers of the First World War, an Encyclopaedia*, p708 Garland Publishing. A useful guide to the dates on which the various powers held Odessa. However, Paul's account says that the Whites had two months in Odessa during spring 1919, that are not indicated by either Tucker or Eisfeld.

South Russia. Suggests that "by mid-June, the Reds were chased from the Odessa area," which fits better with Paul's timeline. However, no primary reference is given. So Paul's evidence is the best I have. Available at https://en.wikipedia.org/wiki/Russian_Civil_War (Accessed 8 April 2019)

Vaatz, Albert. F. (Paul's oldest brother) (No date) A handwritten inventory, in blue and purple ink and pencil, of Vaatz estates at Karlovka and elsewhere. Provides detailed evidence (down to the numbers of sheep and buckets) of the land ownership and wealth of the Vaatz family. When the family fled Russia, there were eight large Vaatz estates in the region, and this ignores the property of female descendants of the line. Albert's notes were perhaps drafted when he was claiming his share of the compensation that the German state was paying the *Russlandeutschen* (Russian-Germans) out of funds received from the Bolsheviks to compensate those who had lost their property. Private collection.

Vaatz, Alexander (1942) *Deutsche Bauernarbeit im Schwarzmeergebiet* [German Farm Management in the Black Sea Region], Verlag C.V. Engelhard. Alexander is recorded as having been killed in the Second World War. While his book provides evidence of the living style, methods and successes of German farmers in the region, its purpose seems to be to seek the support of the German state and its occupying forces for the *Russlanddeutschen.* The year of publication is that following the occupation of Odessa by German troops in WW2.

Vaatz, Arnold (2017) *Stammbaum der Familie Vaatz* [The Vaatz family tree] Private communication.

Vaatz, Paul A. (December1938) *Der Bolschevik – Selbsterlebnise Odessa u. Umgebung in 1919* [The Bolsheviks – My life in Odessa and its surroundings during 1919] Typed with handwritten annotations. The primary source for the structure and many details of this story. Private collection.

Vaatz, Paul A. (1938) *Die Schilderung der Einwanderung unserer Familie Vaatz im Jahre 1834, aus Deutschland nach Russland* [An account of the immigration of the family Vaatz from Germany to

Russia in 1834] Typewritten document. It is interesting to note that the above two pieces were written in the same year that the Kristallnacht took place, one before and one after the event. It is not clear why Paul chose to write at this time, some nineteen years after his arrival in Germany. Private collection.

Vaatz, Paul A. (1918) Annotated photo of Paul and two Vaatz cousins evidencing that they were demobbed from their German regiment in Graudenz (present-day Romania). I assume that they enrolled, not long before, during the German occupation of Odessa in March 1918 and offered themselves as interpreters. They may have joined earlier, soon after the Bolshevik and the German governments made peace in December1917. This photograph is annotated with the names of eight Vaatzs who died 'fighting at the front.' It is not clear whether fighting for the White (Tsarist) - or the German – army. Private collection.

Vaatz, Paul A. (1920) Red Cross Travel document granting the Vaatz family free rail travel to Stuttgart, the location of the Mercedes-Benz HQ. Private collection.

Vaatz, Sophia (1917) Postcard from Sophia at home in Odessa to daughter Tamara on holiday at the farm estate of her Uncle Albert, giving news of meetings between local landowners, farmers and peasants in Odessa following the 1917 uprisings in the north. She also asks Tamara to be more respectful to the governess. Private collection.

General reading

Dwinger, Edwin Erich (1930) *Zwischen Weiss und Rot.* Eugen Diederichs Verlag Jena. [Between White and Red] The harrowing story of a White Russian-German junior officer fighting with General

Kolchak in the eastern Russian campaigns. Given to Isa for Christmas when she was sixteen.

Foley, Michael. (1918) *Russian Civil War, History of Terror.* Pen and Sword Military. ISBN 978 1 52678 61 6.

Hodgson, John E. (1932) *With Denikin's Armies: Being a Description of the Cossack Counter-Revolution in South Russia, 1918-1920",* Temple Bar Publishing Co., London, pp. 54-56.

"I had not been with Denikin more than a month before I was forced to the conclusion that the Jew represented a very big element in the Russian upheaval. The officers and men of the Army laid practically all the blame for their country's troubles on the Hebrew. They held that the whole cataclysm had been engineered by some great and mysterious secret society of international Jews, who, in the pay and at the orders of Germany, had seized the psychological moment and snatched the reins of government. All the figures and facts that were then available appeared to lend colour to this contention. No less than 82 per cent of the Bolshevik Commissars were known to be Jews, the fierce and implacable 'Trotsky,' who shared office with Lenin, being a Yiddisher whose real name was Bronstein. Among Denikin's officers this idea was an obsession of such terrible bitterness and insistency as to lead them into making statements of the wildest and most fantastic character."

Hodgson was War Correspondent with the Anti-Bolshevik Forces. This evidence of the intense anti-Semitism of the Russian bourgeoisie is re-quoted in several references relating to the Russian Revolution.

Marullo, Thoma Gaiton. (1998) *Cursed Days: Evan Bunin.* Ivan R. Dee, Chicago. ISBN 1-56663-186-6.

Kenez, Peter (1977) *Civil War in South Russia, 1919-1920*: *The defeat of the Whites.* University of California. ISBN 0-520-03346-9.

Kort, Michael. (2010)*The Soviet Colossus,* Routledge.

Mc Meekin, Sean (2018) *The Russian Revolution: A New History.* CPI Group UK. ISBN 978 1 78125 903 0.

Popoff, Georg. (1925) *TsCheKa* (in German), Frankfurter Societäts – Druckerei. [CheKa] Isa was given this book by 'Mama & Papa,' in its year of publication, when she was only fifteen. Its description of the tortures inflicted by the CheKa makes a challenging read.

Rappaport, Helen. (2016) *Caught in the Revolution*, Hutchison.

Rachmanova, Alexandra (1931) *Studenten liebe Tscheka und Tod.* Universitäts-Buchdruckerei 'Styria'. Graz. [Student love, the Cheka and death] Presented to Isa when she was twenty-six.

Richardson, Tanya. (2008) Kaleidoscopic Odessa. University of Toronto Press. ISBN 978-0-8020-9563-3

Service, Robert. (2017) *The last of the Tsars*, Macmillan. ISBN 978-1-4472-9309-5.

Sifineos, Evrydiki. (2018) *Imperial Odessa: Peoples, Spaces, Places*, Brill.

Smele, Jonathan, D. (2017) *The "Russian" Civil Wars "1916-1926*, Oxford University Press. ISBN 9780190861148.

Smith, Douglas (2012) *Former People: The Last Days of the Russian Aristocracy.* Pan MacMillan. ISBN 978-0-330-52029-4.

Vaatz Witold (1934?) *Unter Räubern in der Krim* [Among thieves in the Crimea] Junge Generation Verlag, Berlin.

Printed in Poland
by Amazon Fulfillment
Poland Sp. z o.o., Wrocław